DICTATORS

DICTATORS

Peter Vansittart

Studio Vista London

To Constance

Acknowledgements
I am most grateful for help and information from Mr Eric Rhode, Mr Gerry Graber, Mr Kyril Fitzlyon, Ken and Valerie Minogue. To James Laver and his work on Nostradamus, and to Herr Odd Nansen for his drawings a special word is necessary. Acknowledgements are due to Mrs Sonia Orwell and Secker and Warburg for permission to quote from the late George Orwell; to Mr Ezra Pound and Faber and Faber for permission to quote from the Cantos of Ezra Pound; to the late J. B. Leishman and Chatto and Windus for quotations from Rainer Maria Rilke.

I wish to thank the following for help and permission for the illustrations: Mr Fred Uhlman, Mr Renzo Galeotti, Miss Josephine Crickmay, Mr A. S. Neill. The illustrations on pages 18, 19, 20, 24, 44, 45, 61, 68, 86, 134, 138 are reproduced by permission of the Trustees of the British Museum; on page 51 by permission of the Kupferstichkabinett, Dresden; on page 52, the Kupferstichkabinett, Staatliche Museum, Berlin; pages 11, 29, 30, 64, 88, 90, 94 *below*, 95, London Associated Press; pages 82, 84, 89, 143, the trustees of David Low and the *Evening Standard*; pages 23, 57, 71, Marlborough Fine Art (London); pages 6, 8, 9, *below*, 10, 15, 22, 26, 27, 32, 34, 35, 36, 42, 59, 118, 126, 131, 132, 133, the National Film Archive, London; pages 55, 78, 79, the Prado, Madrid; pages 25, 83, 121, 123, 124, 128, 130, 135, 142, the Tate Gallery, London; page 75, the Musée de Versailles; pages 101, 103, 105, 108, 109, 111, 113, 117, the Victoria and Albert Museum, London, Crown Copyright Reserved. The illustrations from *Captivity* are reproduced by permission of Jonathan Cape Ltd; those from *Day after Day* by permission of Dreyers Forlag, Oslo, and Putnam, London; the one from *Zaharoff the Armaments King* by permission of Allen and Unwin; and that from *Urania's Children* by permission of William Kimber Ltd.

The list is woefully incomplete, but should there be any vital acknowledgement due, the author will be happy to be contacted by those concerned.

(hardback) ISBN 0 289 70313 1
(paperback) ISBN 0 289 70431 6

Photoset in 11 point Ehrhardt and printed by
BAS Printers Limited, Wallop, Hampshire

Contents

The abuse of greatness is when it disjoins
Remorse from Power.

Shakespeare

Whoever wishes to organize a State and
establish its laws must presuppose that
all men are mad.

Machiavelli

Neither man nor woman can be worth
anything until they have discovered that
they are fools. This is the first step towards becoming either estimable or agree-
able; and until it is taken there is no hope.
The sooner the discovery is made the
better, as there is more time and power
for taking advantage of it. Sometimes the
great truth is found out too late to apply
to it any effectual remedy. Sometimes it is
never found at all, and these form the
desperate and inveterate causes of human
folly, self-conceit and impertinence.

Lord Melbourne

When God raises up such men as Caesar,
Charlemagne and Napoleon, it is to trace
the way that people ought to follow, to
stamp a new era with the seal of their
genius. Woe to those who misunderstand
and combat them. They do as the Jews
did, they crucify their Messiah.

Napoleon III

Perpetual peace is a dream, and not even
a beautiful dream . . . In War are developed
the noblest virtues of humanity. Without
War the world would be swallowed up in
materialism.

Field Marshal von Moltke

Nothing beyond the State, above the
State, against the State. Everything to the
State, for the State, in the State.

Mussolini

There is a great tide of good-nature and
comprehension in civilized mankind which
sweeps to and fro and washes all the
pebbles against each other, cleanses the
beach of sea-weed, strawberry baskets
and lobster-pots. Hurrah for the tide!

Winston Churchill

I am freeing men from the tiresome
restrictions of the mind, from the duty
and degrading self-mortification of a
chimera called conscience and morality,
and from the demands of a freedom and
personal independence which only a few
will experience.

Adolf Hitler

Most of you will know what it means to
see a hundred dead bodies, five hundred,
a thousand lying there. But seeing the
matter through and nevertheless, save for
a few exceptions due to human failings,
remaining decent, that is what has made
us hard. This is a never told and never to
be told page of glory in our history.

Heinrich Himmler

The Jews should have offered themselves
to the butcher's knife. They should have
thrown themselves into the sea from cliffs.
It would have aroused the world and the
German people.

Mahatma Gandhi

There never was a man so varied, so rich,
so fruitful, so omnipotent a genius . . .
He astounds by his wisdom, by the
irreproachable correctness of his advice to
masters of every trade. There is in all the
world no other man who can see so clearly
as Stalin does. His forecasts are without
error. Stalin's genius opens for us novel
and grand vistas. Yes, the People's adora-
tion for Stalin is unlimited, for Stalin is
our life and our victory. Stalin is our
great Destiny.

Pravda

From *Ivan the Terrible* 1944. Ivan invokes God, yet
seems himself the superhuman figure Russia has
often assented to, or craved

Part I
The God-like Dictator

Louis Gaugey *Avant la Guerre* contemporary.
Napoleon III as a peacock

I believe that periodically men are created whom I will call heaven-sent, in whose hands their country's destinies are placed. I believe myself to be one of those men.

Napoleon III

The archetypal dictator is a dream-figure summoned by longings vague but innumerable. Often he has a wretched childhood, inadequate father, or disputed paternity, leaving him with convictions of inferiority, needs for love wrestling with hate and resentment, to be assuaged by action. He emerges from nowhere, or the Underworld, with a few disciples, during breakdown or fears of breakdown. Combining elements of adventurer, warrior, showman, magician, sportshero, tragic hero, buffoon, pied piper, charmer, salesman, lover, he unites contradictory interests. He is welcomed by the rich as restorer of order, by the mob for his sensationalism. He has the attractions, both daring and fatalistic, of a gambler. He tears power from an exhausted régime, or from idealists whose moral passions are unaccompanied by administrative ability or ruthlessness. Promising miracles, he slays the monster—street fights, inflation, political turmoil, demoralization—takes the kingdom, initiates reforms, through force. If Life is sacred, lives are not. But he dare not admit that the emergency is over. With further miracles breathlessly expected he must continue, robbing people of identity on pretence of restoring it, so that they need him, the permanent, indispensable rain-maker, as urgently as, drugged by his own glamour, he needs himself.

He often shirks the drabness of regular administration, so cannot shed repression. Grandiose schemes are not always completed. Histrionics, intuition, intrigue, propaganda, outbid tact, delegation, routine.

8

He is like one who enjoys saying 'Mozart' but is bored by music. He seeks increasing despotism, spiritual and practical, for the miracle to ensure his fortunes for ever. The most simple and enthralling is that of renewed violence, at home or abroad. Usually he fails, leaving disasters worse than those he originally sought to remedy. He may die in sacrificial flame or by a form of hanging; he may mysteriously vanish, or die on a foreign shore, though perhaps enjoying posthumous resurrection. He has been crucified by the contradictions between his divinity, his promise of the Kingdom, and his role of a man with a job to do. The contradictions, however, may ensure his survival in the vast territories of dream and unconscious ritual: an infinity of bellowing silence.

Alison Morgan *The Magician in Legend* 1971

From *Yellow Caesar* 1941. Shot of Mussolini from Cavalcanti's 'documentary'

The Unchanging Mind

All History is Contemporary History.

Croce

When there was peace, he was for peace, when there was War, he went.

W. H. Auden

From *The Triumph of the Will* 1937. This film swiftly conveys the overwhelming, sometimes supernatural effect of dictatorship on undernourished minds, and not on them alone

We may forget the Past, the Past does not forget us. Here conspirators took counsel, a mock-king was crowned in the market-place: there a criminal or slave scratched his mark, there men marched. Body and mind, however, at the nerve-ends of millennia, keep less tangible memories, scars, obsessions.

In this perspective the real Revolution—Upright Stance, Agriculture, Language—has

long occurred: no subsequent convulsion has altered human nature, so is scarcely revolution at all. Throughout history, human energies are collected by identical heroes and devils, princesses and magicians. Since 1789 France has had four 'revolutions', at least ten régimes: none has significantly changed actual Frenchmen.

'You are young, you Westerners,' a Chinese diplomat informed Flaubert. 'You have scarcely any history to speak of . . . It has always been like this . . . the Siege and Commune are everyday events for the human race.' (*Goncourt Journals*)

Power, violence, free-will are to-day being energetically debated. Some emphasize human descent from an ill-natured ape: others, peaceful cooperation amongst animals, whose violence is usually defensive, a last resort preceded by elaborate bluff. Others reject all animal analogies.

Significant in man is his capacity not only for war but also for acting against his immediate interests: he will vote proposals that will double his own taxes: will support the weaker team against his own, for the good of the game.

Here, the majority will be held as neither inherently aggressive nor slavish, very good nor very bad, but as rather lazy, a bundle of pontentials, often unconscious until challenged by drastic change or thrilling individual. A youth, nervous and timid because of his Slavonic name, Dyga, became transformed into a savage SS killer at Lwow–Janowska Camp (Wiesenthal). Hitler confessed that, at the age of twenty-five, he yearned for a life in which he could 'respect his superior, contradict no one, blindly obey'. Frustrations have bred criminal and saint.

Those who see man as a cipher controlled by God or unconscious animal pressures will accept authority more wholeheartedly than those who, in practical affairs, resist what they may academically accept. A leader who rejects the impersonal and dehumanizing can be sure of a hearing.

Man is not yet a formula. 'I once found in a book of migration particulars of an Indian

Mosley at Blackshirt Parade 1936

tribe deep in the deepest, remotest jungle inside Brazil, who gave way every so often to a desire to look at the sea. They travelled thousands of miles through swamps and trees and down the Amazon, and looked at the Atlantic, and came back.' (Geoffrey Grigson, *Notes from an Odd Country*) This could instance curiosity specifically human, or blind animal instinct, or complex marriage of both.

The career of Oswald Mosley, once Britain's would-be dictator, successively Conservative, Labour, New Party, Fascist, warns against over-simplification. Mosley possessed idealism, unusual intelligence, arrogance, personal courage, self-deceit. Character seems a maze of opposites thriving on disputes. Not only a Nero, Wallenstein, Laval is superstitious: Zola, Freud, like Mussolini, were fascinated and alarmed by certain recurring numbers. Years of official atheism may have strengthened Russian religion. The gentle Mozart rejoiced that 'that godless arch-rascal Voltaire has pegged out like a dog'. (*Letters*, 3 July 1788) Kurt Gerstein (1942) both supplied the Auschwitz SS with prussic acid for exterminations and tried to sabotage the system and betray it to the outside world.

Man, whether grappling with neolithic

axe or cybernetics, desires incompatibles: solitude, and blaring cities: adventure, yet security: marriage and wildness: idealism and grossness: extravagance and economy. He desires to conquer the beloved and to be abased: to be cherished by authority and sacrificed to it: to be civilized, yet utterly free. He evokes gods of mischief, disorder, evil, to upset the monotony and dangers of too perfect a pattern. Boredom has as many teeth as a colony of rats: planting time-bombs in marriage and régime, inciting aggressive howls for love and peace in expensive colleges. Psychic conflicts make the shy dream violence. Man secretly rejoices at his hero's downfall, his friend's misfortune; wants to beat his favourite wife and be ravaged by Cingalese Fourth Mates: desires to be rocket and dormouse. Like the bored Hampshire firemen (1971)—like a Dictator— he starts fires in order to put them out. 'Not only would I be happy to be a victim, but I would not even hate to be an executioner, so as to feel the Revolution from both sides.' (Baudelaire)

This stew of impulses transcends class, race, education, progress. Contemporary people are seldom modern. Alfonso XIII of Spain (1886–1941) was widely believed amongst all classes in Spain and Italy to have 'the Evil Eye'. The huge Donati comet, 1858, was regarded throughout Europe as presaging war, which indeed occurred next year, with Napoleon III's invasion of Italy. Irrationality, once attributed to Dionysus, Satan, original sin, provokes the fruitful, the destructive. Dissonances are essential, in music, in love, in debate. Seneca speaks of the opposites inherent in things; to Heraclitus, Conflict was the Father of all. Man seeks conflict—admirable as stimulus, dangerous as goal—not necessarily to loot but to avoid stagnation. For William Morris, whom Shaw considered the saint of the century, 'Men fight and lose the battle, and the thing they fight for comes about in spite of their defeat, and when it comes turns out to be not what they meant, and other men have to fight for what they meant under another name.'

War solves few public problems and, as for the young Hitler (1914) too many personal ones. 'There must be more fighting. You ask why? Merely to make a name for us.' (Frederick the Great, admirer of Voltaire) The Volscian servants in *Coriolanus* find war a ravisher, peacemaking men hate each other. 'This peace is nothing but to rust iron, increase tailors and breed ballad-mongers.' 'Tranquillity,' said Lloyd George, 'is not a policy, it's a yawn.'

War origins appear more complex than their former packet-explanations: capitalist contradictions and rivalry between arms firms: the affluence deriving from a war-economy: struggle for oil, nitrates, markets: thwarted sexuality: too strict toilet training of functionaries. Perhaps man, physically not very formidable, relying on brain rather than claw, had to develop both his creative and destructive potential the more thoroughly, but defective social organization should never be disregarded. People of New Guinea were savage and cannibal, those of Timur peaceful and musical. Contemporary Danes contrast with their Viking ancestors. That Bolivia has had 187 risings since 1824 and Switzerland none suggests political rather than biological promptings. Tribes exist, as in Assam, with women dominant and martial, men gentle, contented with weaving, pottery, cooking.

Nevertheless, violence and pain have remained a perennial and ambiguous court of appeal. A smile may be a spontaneous gift of personality, means of defence, or calculated act of aggression. Man may fight bravely because he is too cowardly not to, the mind be troubled by too much repose. 'Happiness,' said Stendhal, 'is where I am not.' The passionate, humanitarian Dickens was yet obsessed with crime and hangings, 'the attraction of repulsion', which gave Conrad's Marlowe an appalled thrill when he heard savages howling in the heart of darkness. The Little Mermaid gladly walked on blades. Not only the Mongol conquerors but the Salvationist is quickened by Blood and Fire.

Such duality makes life more interesting,

less controllable. System-mongers and legislators frequently forget that, in the unconscious, fair is foul, foul is fair, liars speak truth and man loves what he hates. Winston Churchill (28 July 1914) wrote to his wife:

Everything tends towards catastrophe and collapse. I am interested, geared up and happy. Is it not horrible to be built like that? The preparations have a hideous fascination for me. I pray to God to forgive me for such fearful moods of levity. Yet I wd do my very best for peace and nothing wd induce me wrongfully to strike the blow.

Man has an inclination ever to strengthen authority, then trust to luck. He is credulous. Roger Bacon traced human ignorance to believing the written word without evidence, to accepting majority opinion on trust, to preferring the glib and specious to the hard work of truth, to obeying fashion. A new Revolution will occur when this analysis by a thirteenth-century monk is rendered nonsense.

The Mind's Tendency to Look Backwards

The Ballad grew perfect by a kind of forgetting.

Edwin Muir

Human kind cannot bear too much reality.

T. S. Eliot

Two souls, alas, dwell within my breast.

Goethe

Human energies roam fiercely round bases apparently constant. Sacrifice, sacrament, coronation, election, crusade, cup-final are practical gadgets for visible results but also the expression of varied emotional needs. To escape facts, improve status, protect property, to avoid loneliness, from fear of darkness, man invents fantasies, drenched with imageries from the past.

History is a blank cheque for the imagination. It is often easier to write a historical novel than convincing science fiction or practical utopia. Ancient heroes have the advantage of speaking only by exaggerated deeds or words given them by major poets. Their own words, or grunts, are lost, perhaps fortunately. Silence breeds gods. It is easier, Lytton Strachey reflected, for a lady to fall in love with her footman if she is deaf. Lord Melbourne considered that classical literature is considered so good because so much of it is lost. Too much history, however, is invented by the unscrupulous. The Papacy did not disdain forgery of historical evidence and precedent. Papal Elections, often unseemly brawls, were officially influenced by the Holy Ghost, not always wisely. Benedict IX (1083), aged, perhaps, twelve, sold the office for cash, only to retrieve it later. With some relish Gibbon observes the arrest of 'John XXIII', one of three rival Popes. 'The

most scandalous charges were suppressed: the Vicar of Christ was only accused of piracy, murder, rape, sodomy and incest.' (*Decline and Fall of the Roman Empire*)

Winston Churchill considered mankind 'unteachable from infancy to the tomb'. Certainly the past is played like cards, manipulated by cynical conjurors. 'We have created our myth, it is not necessary that it should be a reality.' (Mussolini, 1927)

Mussolini filled schools with 'Italy won the (1914–18) War at the Battle of Vitorio Veneto'. Stalin had the Russian Revolution rewritten, omitting Trotsky, as his successors omit Khrushchev. Napoleon I at St Helena sedulously reinterpreted his career as that of a pacific liberal internationalist with the French as the wronged ones, a view republished by Napoleon III. Gustavus Adolphus of Sweden justified his invasion of Germany as 'reclaiming' lands and natural rights stolen from his ancestors, 'the Goths'. Maoist historians totally erase the former hero, Liu Shao-Chi, transferring many of his exploits to 'our most respected and beloved Great Leader, Chairman Mao'. A French pamphlet against Napoleon III was transformed, probably by Tsarist police officials, into 'The Protocols of the Elders of Zion', to justify pogroms by revealing a Jewish world-conspiracy, a fantasy that entranced Hitler, and, for a time, convinced Tsar Nicholas II, Henry Ford, *The Times*, the *Spectator*, bishops, Ludendorff.

Commercial and psychological needs can change a hen-witted waitress and a minor homosexual thief into 'Bonnie and Clyde', resourceful and athletic lovers, inviting sympathy, to whom murder is a style of wit. A small-time pimp, Horst Wessel, became a Nazi martyr: Marx and Lenin remain ikons. The bare past is continually reissued as the grand or grandiose. Dazzled by the past, man seeks traditional authority as he does bread, warmth, a mate, so that the Caesars are deified, Alexander is hailed, and hails himself 'Son of Jupiter'. Himmler revered Hitler as an avatar-messiah, with himself as the reincarnation of Henry the Lion, medieval King of Saxony, with whose spirit he would regularly commune. At Wewelsburg Castle he had a Round Table, 100 feet by 145, at which to entertain twelve SS paladins. The founder of the Chinese Republic, Sun Yat-Sen, is worshipped as a god in Formosa: in Outer Japan are Shintoist shrines to General MacArthur: Gandhi is liable to be revered as an avatar of Vishnu. Certain Japanese torturers in wartime Burma claimed to be Buddhists, though Buddha,

From *Niebelungen Saga* 1923

who never claimed divinity, deplored violence even to a vegetable.

Ritual and authority cease to be reasoned devices for better government and emotional stability and are etherealized to talismans. The Party, the Revolution, the Holy Places, God's Will, Private Property, the Republic, the Crown, the Fatherland, can degenerate into superstitions of mastery or slavery. Like magical incantations, they dissolve civilized or over-civilized good sense. The Revolution, Camus noted, becomes more important than those it wishes to save. Henry V ascribed the Agincourt carnage to God punishing the sins of the French. 'Deus vult', howled the First Crusaders, who were to wade to Christ's Tomb through streets awash with massacre.

The sanctity of Property has curious embellishments. In his *George VI*, John Wheeler-Bennet writes of World War II:

When Mr Leopold Amery proposed to the Air Minister that, in view of Germany's shortage of timber, some attempt should be made to set fire to the Black Forest, Sir Kingsley Wood replied that there was no question of the RAF bombing even the munition works at Essen, 'which were private property'.

In South Australia, June 1965, a Jehovah's Witness preferred to die in childbirth rather than accept blood-transfusion, against God's Word. Tolstoy and Gandhi would have approved.

Imagination has limitless need to mythologize governments, events, changes, into familiar heroes, saviours, scapegoats, victims, monsters, devils and traitors, fallen angels and ascending souls. A people draining a marsh may be remembered as a hero slaying a dragon; Death envisaged as a live skeleton; Liberty a moist young woman.

In 1389 the Turks defeated the Serbs at Kossovo, the Field of Blackbirds.

Mankind has devised a number of ways of dealing with the bitter fact of military defeat. The least noble is to try and ignore it by using some kind of drug; the most noble, perhaps, is to decide that defeat is actually for the best, to immerse in the destructive element. That is how the Serbs dealt with their defeat at Kossovo. Far from seeking to ignore it they have made it the centre of their legends, feigning, for instance, in their ballads, that before the battle a dove sent by God from Jerusalem, asked King Lazarus whether he would choose victory and success in this life, or defeat, and glory in the next world; and he chose defeat.

E. M. Tillyard

In darker relief, Wilhelm II and Hitler both maintained that Germany was undefeated in 1918, merely betrayed by Jews and Socialists. 'That race of criminals has on its conscience the two million (German) corpses of World War I, and now hundreds of thousands more.' (Hitler, 1941)

The language of power transcends Time.

'May your sentence of death hit them like an iron fist, without any pity. May your sentence be a fire, burning out this treacherous growth to its roots. Your sentence should ring like a bell through our glorious Fatherland, a signal for new victories.'

Is this Ancient or Modern? Left or Right? Christian, Pagan, Atheist? Uttered by Ashur-bani-Pal of Assyria, by Goering? Actually, by the Public Prosecutor at the Slansky Show Trial, Prague, 1952.

Extremists, despite their glamorous tomorrows, perpetually hark backwards: Anabaptists to Primitive Christianity, Levellers to an imaginary pre-Norman Golden Age, Jacobins to Sparta and Republican Rome, Fascists to Imperial Rome, Nazis to the Germania of Woden and Hermann that overwhelmed Augustus' legions. Napoleon I and III were New Caesars, the latter eulogizing Julius.

Superficially the Marxists have disowned superstitions but they too canonize and distort such events as the French Revolution and Paris Commune, and propagate the class-conflict as a self-righteous, inexorable, old-fashioned Crusade, which excuses all extremes of behaviour on its behalf. The literal has irresistible gravitation towards the poetic. One must, stated Adolf Hitler, become a dreamer to become a ruler. People are continually betrayed, blackmailed, tricked by heroes whom they support beyond the limit, under such exuberant but finally meaningless slogans as 'Strength through Joy', even 'Long Live Death'.

Josephine Crickmay *Heraldic Eagle* 1971

Magic and Power

Lintel *c*. AD 709, from Ancient Maya Ceremonial Centre at Menche, Guatemala, showing a penitent kneeling before a priest and mutilating his tongue by passing a rope of thorns through it.

But the greatest thing of all, by far, is to be a master of metaphor. It is the one thing that cannot be learned from others; and it is also a sign of original genius, since a good metaphor implies the instinctive perception of the similarity in dissimilars.

Aristotle

Magic and power are inextricably entwined. Like music, like moonlight, absolute power seems a flight to the ends of the earth, appealing more to intuition than intelligence. Though capable of manic spells of hard work, a Hitler is slovenly, more eager to exploit archaic dreams and daydreams. He assumes Magic more readily than do hereditary rulers: having to strain for the sceptre, not passively inherit it, he must continually display it.

Power requires trickery. Roman priests released an eagle from the dead Emperor's pyre, as the soul rising to heaven. Statues of Gods, Virgins, saints which agitate heads or hands have been commonplace. Continually the imagination wavers between real and unreal.

For children and primitives, toys, jugs, statues, trees, fire, animals, the dark, are human, to be enjoyed, placated, threatened. The infant is absorbed with his own body and his powers over it: also with his parents, gods who tyrannize, on whom he depends, yet, to achieve growth, must increasingly resist. Fantasies of love and hate, magic and omnipotence, swiftly entangle him, together with catastrophic disappointments, resentments, and bewilderments, when magic fails. Similarly, the adult feels, or suppresses, ambiguous feelings about gods and society. The Unconscious, electric mass of possi-

Aphrodite Riding on a Bird 470–60 BC

bility, makes history as readily as does Napoleon, and assists in breeding the Napoleonic. 'We must dream', Lenin cried to the Assembly.

The child watches Punch and Judy, and wonders what they do in the dark after the theatre is closed. Perhaps they enjoy the monstrous. Hamlet, Odysseus, Robin Hood outlive William Pitt. Himmler, and H. S. Chamberlain, prophet of Teutonic racialism, believed in literal devils.

Language enables all to share and expand fantasies, as well as explode them. For Hitler, 'the broad masses of the people can be moved only by the power of speech'. Through language man masters the world. 'Blue is the colour of thy yellow hair,' wrote Schwitters. Words extract souls from stones, enchant mobs, transform the commonplace to art, man to superman. God, like the Dictator, continually swaps masks: Avenging Judge, Kindly Father, Protector of the Weak, Colleague of the Strong. The sun becomes an Egyptian sky-boat, Persian swastika-talisman, handsome Greek youth, an Aztec mouth greedy for victims. Hill-tops are haunted by invisible presences. Man sees very clearly fussy household gods, spectres of the rose, elegant snobbish unicorns.

George Barker's remark that the unicorns do not exist because they have better things to do, exploits the full powers of language. Therein is Man's glory, therein is a map of hell. Man plucks from himself not only Orpheus but Moloch: Apollo can be generous and radiant, or coldly vicious. Man makes ornate demands for other people's pain and sometimes for his own.

Dictators are lords of metaphor, or slaves to it. In the dark twists of power, subject may

King Darius in his Chariot Hunting Lions c. 500 BC

be confused with object, words lose concrete meaning, connection with social needs, so that Franco's Falangists bellowed 'Long Live Death', and the Jacobin Barère insisted that true humanity consists in exterminating one's enemies. 'Rome went to pot when it was no longer the fashion to hit the nail on the head.' (Ezra Pound)

Political hooligans do not monopolize verbal inflation. When Walter Scott lamented 'an act of wickedness more surely diabolical than any hitherto upon record', few will at once recognize his reference to the publication of the *Complete Works of Lord Bolingbroke*. But dictatorship notably assists life as collision between white Knights and black Satanists, is hypnotized not by the content but the sound of words, which collapse into music. St Augustine had praised words as 'precious cups of meaning'. Too often drunk on sounds, the Dictator is left swaying over a cup, gleaming, jewelled, but empty of meaning. John of Leyden, Jacobins, Nazis, used words as spells, en-

trapping themselves as thickly as their followers. 'The Revolutionary Government is the Despotism of Freedom against Tyranny.' (Robespierre) 'Conscience is a Jewish invention, a blemish like circumcision.' (Hitler) For Himmler the extermination of Jews was 'an act of hygiene'. An SS motto was 'My Honour is my Loyalty'. Dr Johnson supplies the epitaph: 'Truth, sir, is a cow that will yield such people no milk, so they are gone to milk the bull.'

Man believes what he wants to believe, so that government is as much theatre as office. People will accept the Protocols of Zion, hold that Stonehenge was a port for Flying Saucers, that Lenin was a Jew, that God lives in Cambridge. In 1967 an Egyptian professor claimed Shakespeare an Iraki, Sheik Subir. Shakespeare, like Jesus, Napoleon, Lenin, is a catalyst for energetic but conflicting theorists. Delia Bacon went mad enunciating (1856) that the plays, 'a standing disgrace to genius and learning', were written by a syndicate to promote democratic revolution: Dr Owen perfected (1894) a machine to prove that Francis Bacon, son of Elizabeth and Leicester, murdered Shakespeare while resisting blackmail. Cromwell massacred the Irish, convinced that he was fulfilling God's Will. Marx's vision of the Classless Society erected on proletarian virtue derived not from observation of people but from the symmetries of theory. 'Not even the lowest liar on the BBC has claimed that Hitler started it (the War)', Ezra Pound declared (7 December 1941). Oswald Mosley claimed, 'Before the organization of the Blackshirt movement, Free Speech did not exist in this country [Britain].' Ramdöhr, Political Chief of Ravensbrück Camp, exterminated thousands but regarded himself as 'Protector of the Poor and Oppressed'.

Historical villains and heroes are swollen on misshapen memories. Graham Greene (*Observer*, 26 October 1969) wrote of 'the face of Lord Haig whom I saw as a pall-bearer at the funeral of Rudyard Kipling—a face flushed probably with indigestion but it looked like make-up, a look of savage stupidity and deep lines as cruel as the trenches of the Somme.' Yet Kipling died in 1936, Haig in 1928. Make-believe is fostered by ignorance. Not Marie Antoinette but the thirteenth-century Archbishop Peckham wondered why the poor did not eat cake:

From *The Triumph of the Will* 1937

ironically castigating the gulf between rich and poor. Illiterate Russians (1825) cheered 'Constantine and Constitution', imagining them man and wife.

Prejudices enlarge with false rumour. Medieval continentals had disposition to believe that Englishmen were born with tails, particularly in East Anglia. Education Acts do not exorcise beliefs in magic, witchcraft, ghosts: children remain scared of Jack the Ripper, the Black Man, Winnie with the Long Green Fingers. An English schoolboy wrote (1945): 'Jesus Christ was the man who went on a secret mission into the East. The gestapo captured and hung him under a yellow star. But were not allowed to torture him. After three days dead he came back and the old dog died of joy.'

Courts, royal or dictatorial, tend to welcome clairvoyants, seers, magicians, faith-healers, Nostradamus or Rasputin, solace for those sated with too much power or scared by too little, all needing to sidestep 'the regular channels'. Spiritualism and astrology flourished with Hitler and Mussolini, as with Nicolas II and Napoleon III, Hitler employing a Swiss astrologer, Ernst Krafft.

Occultists helped find the captured Mussolini and, less successfully, allied shipping. The planet Pluto, discovered 1930, was hailed by astrologers as 'the cosmic aspect originating the Third Reich.' (Ellic Howe, *Urania's Children*)

Alternately dominant or recessive, Astrological Time accompanies Calendar Time, enriching the drift towards dictators, myths, omens, fear of the Lord. The Nazis, as Orwell put it, used science on behalf of superstition. Of the murder of the German-Jewish Foreign Minister, Walter Rathenau (1922), Norman Cohn in *Warrant for Genocide* writes: 'Rathenau was not simply assassinated as an Elder of Zion, he was offered up as a human sacrifice to the sun-god of ancient Germanic religion. The murder was timed to coincide with the Summer Solstice; and when the news was published, young Germans gathered on hill-tops to celebrate simultaneously the turning of the year and the destruction of one who symbolized the powers of darkness.' The German film *The Triumph of the Will* (1937) showed Hitler as redeemer, descending from clouds.

The Sacredness of Authority

There was a look in their faces which showed both that they were born to command and that none of their commands would ever be any good to anybody.
Lytton Strachey

I do not know much about gods; but I think that the river is a strong brown god . . .
T. S. Eliot

I can only be grateful to Providence that it entrusted me with the leadership in this historic struggle which, for the next five hundred or a thousand years, will be decisive not only for the history of Germany but for all Europe and indeed the entire world. A historical revision on a scale unprecedented has been inspired on us by the Creator.   Adolf Hitler
(declaring war on USA, 1941)

Britain is inclined to judge other peoples by the standards of parliamentary democracy, which few have ever experienced or show much willingness to imitate sincerely. Plato would have preferred a Philosopher-King, Dante an Emperor-Messiah, each appealing more deeply to the psyche than rationalists used to admit.

Civilization depends very largely on persuading or compelling people to subscribe for what they do not want. Authority must thus be subtle as well as gaudy, combining the mystical and horrific with the everyday. Early civilization required more centralization, to develop irrigation, calendars, war, public buildings, sacrifices: to confer with gods and neighbours: to protect and reassure illiterates grappling with new complexities of work and thought. Lacking

efficient roads and police, the rulers and priests, sometimes identical, had to impersonate the superhuman with visual extravagance, creating aura through the colossal: pyramids, palaces, statues, animal

George Grosz *Saluting* 1923

and divine insignia, emblems of sun and planets, sacred mummies, robes, magic crowns and weapons. The holy sword, Curtanus, was born in medieval English coronations: Joan knew that Charles was no king unless anointed with the holy oil of Clovis.

Ashur-Nasir-Pal II King of Assyria 883–59 BC. The king being anointed by a magical figure, perhaps a priest, dressed in the head and wings of an eagle.

Kingship and leadership were always religious. Kings expressed the communal soul, as medicine-men ministered to the individual: they were officials, but also sacraments. The sceptre echoed the Magus' Wand, Chinese Emperors sacrificed on behalf of the people. Kings controlled weather and crops, performing sacred marriages at the spring sowing. Roman kings impersonated Jupiter, with oak-leaves and artificial thunder. Joshua, like Merlin, commanded

the sun to obey him. God-kings of Cambodia regulated the dikes.

Mahomet flew on a winged horse, Alborak. Christian Roman Emperors remained 'the Divine Augustus'. The Habsburg Emperor until 1918 was 'Apostolic King' of Hungary, the French King 'Eldest Son of the Church', the Tsar 'Sacred Majesty', the Chinese Emperor 'Son of Heaven'. Dr Johnson was 'touched for the Queen's Evil', residue of royal healing powers. Royal Divine Right lingered into absurdity. 'We Hohenzollerns derive our crowns from Heaven alone and are answerable only to Heaven for the responsibilities they imply.' (Wilhelm II, 1859–1941) General Franco has proclaimed himself 'Responsible only to God and to History'. The Mikado resigned divinity only in 1946. 'Papa Doc' Duvalier, dictator of Haiti, was feared as the human incarnation of Baron Samedi, voodoo guardian of Death's gate. Like many dictators he used spiritual blackmail to impose docility, claiming powers over plants, animals, the dead. During his funeral, May 1971, hysterical mobs panicked at an imaginary earthquake.

The life of society was entangled with that of the King which must be protected by ritual, magic, periodically renewed by sacrifice. Twentieth-century Dinka Kings in East Africa were killed when virility diminished: in the 1950s the King of the Nigerian Junkus was still killed, or had to kill himself, after seven years' reign. Stately chess-like movements both imitated and regulated the cosmic rhythms, some kings always being carried, in fear that, if their feet touched ground, the sacred vibrations would cause earthquake. Byzantine Emperors rode motionless, like hierophantic images.

While the Ambassador bowed down before the Presence, his forehead touching the ground, the throne would slowly rise and he would lift his eyes again to find the Emperor seated high above him, and at the same time the golden lions that flanked the throne would roar and wave their tails and the jewelled birds that sat in the gold and silver trees would open their beaks and sing.

Steven Runciman, *A History of the Crusades*
When Flaubert visited the Holy Sepulchre in Jerusalem he discovered therein a life-sized portrait of King Louis-Philippe.

For dissenters the State promised death, the Church guaranteed hell, an extension of magic that even Hitler or Stalin might have declined. Throne and Altar, rallying cry for centuries, regularized the superstitions of power. The alliance had some surprising conclusions. M. de la Quélen, an Archbishop of Paris, reflected, 'Not only was Jesus Christ the Son of God but he was also of very good family on his mother's side, and

William Blake *The Man who Built the Pyramids* 1819

there are excellent reasons for seeing in him the heir to the throne of Judaea.'

Hugh Thomas in *Cuba* compares Fidel Castro to a priest, interpreting the Revolution. Hitler was officially termed 'a divinely-inspired Leader'. 'Fascism' Mussolini insisted, 'is a religion'.

Authority had to be enhanced by elaborate ceremony: by the splendour of garlanded sacrificial beasts, gilded cypresses, oracular or esoteric speech—when the Emperor of Japan broadcast the surrender, 1946, few understood his court language—occult symbolism, ritual greetings and obeisances: by torches, paintings and sculpture, spectacular executions and ballets, the royal head on coinage: by dogma, hypnotic chants and processions, numbing incense: by fetishes like the Ashanti Gold Stool or the Stone of Scone: by music. Mongol and African leaders had drums 'that spoke', African drum-collections were often sanctuaries. Gongs, trumpets, flutes, together with rhetoric and stylized gestures, induced mindlessness, assent, and stilled positive thinking. 'Men', considered Bertrand Russell, 'fear thought as they fear nothing else—more than ruin, more even than death.'

Elaborate etiquette rendered Authority unearthly, not only in remote Byzantium. During George III's illness, etiquette prevented doctors from questioning him until he himself had spoken, which he sometimes failed to do. Philippe 'Egalité', Jacobin Duke of Orleans, who voted for the killing of his cousin, Louis XVI, was 'not allowed to fix his attention on low objects, as, for instance, servants and dogs'.

Modernity does not expel mysticism; it may, through perversity, man's need to argue, actually increase it. Contemporary radicals are goaded by realization that technology does not of itself produce the Good, the Beautiful, the True, and is more likely to ignore them, perhaps erase them. Communist Hungary still reveres the Crown

From *Niebelungen Saga* 1923

From *The Triumph of the Will* 1937

of St Stephen (at present, 1972, held by the Americans). At Fuerncista, 1937, the Virgin was ordained a Francoist Field Marshal. Latter-day politics seldom wholly transcend magic.

Though man must die, the Hero does not. His holy spirit guarantees the immortality of the faithful. Like Arthur, Charlemagne, Frederick II, T. E. Lawrence, Monmouth, James Dean, he still lives, may return. The Bolsheviks embalmed Lenin for public exhibition as idol, fetish, holy relic, saint.

The more absolute the ruler the more he must both awe and delight. He is careful to present toys, showy though inexpensive, as indeed do all governments. Titles, medals, uniforms make little men feel big. 'What I like about the Garter,' Melbourne confided, 'is that there is no damned merit about it.'

Gibbon has an ominous paragraph on Byzantine Emperors.

To their favourite sons or brothers they imparted the more lofty appellation of Lord or Despot, which was illustrated with new ornaments or prerogatives and placed immediately after the person of the emperor. The five titles of (1) Despot, (2) Sebastocrator, (3) Caesar, (4) Pankypersebastos, (5) Protosebastos, were usually confined to the princes of his blood: they were the emanations of his majesty: but as they exercised no regular function their existence was useless and their authority precarious.

The King of Thailand remains 'Brother of the Moon, Half-Brother to the Sun, Supreme Arbiter of the Ebb and Flow of the Tide, Possessor of the Four and Twenty

Umbrellas'. The latest century has not lacked Duces, Caudillos, Ghazis, Führers, Generalissimos, Redeemers. Russia's highest award is 'Hero of the Soviet Union'. Goering was not only Luftwaffe chief but 'Grand Huntsman of the Reich'. As ruler of Cambodia, Prince Sihanouk was 'My Lord Comrade'. More ambitious was the Dean of the Universe, Dynamo of Salvation, Master of Omnipotence, the American spiritual dictator and preacher, Father Divine, a self-styled immortal, who died, 1965. At a mass-rally, 1936, an old man stood up. 'I propose that Father Divine is God.' This was decreed unanimously—as, 1794, the French revolutionary Convention passed, by majority vote, the existence of the Supreme Being. Years later, 'God' was imprisoned for rape. Four days later the judge died. 'I hated to do it,' said Father Divine.

An embarrassing gap may exist between illusion and reality. Frederick the Great was no hero: Voltaire remarked that the sole recipient of his gratitude was the horse on which he bolted from the field of Mollwitz. 'War is a disciplinary action by God to educate mankind'—thus Wilhelm II, 'Supreme War Lord', looking back to Luther, forward to Mussolini. He informed recruits that, if their Kaiser ordered it, they should fire on their fathers and mothers. During World War I, at Imperial HQ at Spa, miles behind the lines, he had trenches dug and sandbags piled so that he could be photographed 'At the Front'. Hitler and Mussolini spoke like Attila or Napoleon, but, during World War II, avoided the Front and grumbled from safety at other people's efforts. Hitler, Bormann, Himmler, Goebbels, Streicher, Goering, despite the Nazi cult of Aryan supermen, were physically grotesque or mediocre. It is said that when Lord Halifax, aristocratic British Foreign Secretary, first met Hitler (1937) he mistook him for a footman and handed him his hat. The Jacobin scientist-terrorist, Marat, howling for a hundred thousand deaths to preserve the Revolution, was too squeamish even to attend a post-mortem: Napoleon III, 'the

Josephine Crickmay *The Divine Caesar* 1971 drawing from a Roman coin. The deification of Roman emperors, undertaken as political propaganda, at the time may have often seemed ludicrous, but had far-reaching effects, mostly dangerous.

New Caesar', was horrified by an actual battle: Himmler fainted when he at last attended a mass-execution.

Jacobins and Bolsheviks attempted to abolish salutes, gold braid, epaulettes, titles, vainly; man lives by display, by respect for boundaries, by theatre. Uniforms had possessed their own magic since classical heroes paraded in bay wreaths, originally a charm against evil. The riding-breeches sported by Mosley, by Himmler, suggested a Caesar, 'the Man on Horseback'. Uniforms granted immunity, were a spell setting the wearer 'above the Law', or outrider of a rival Law. Crowds were dazzled by the feathers and sashes of men and horses, glittering Guards, jewelled court balls, mock-medieval hunts, the Kremlin's golden domes, the 1400 fountains of Versailles: by the Tsar's gold and white Hussars and Ataman Cossacks in sapphire blue: by the Kaiser's plumed helmet. Napoleon III's court shone with violet masters of ceremony, scarlet chamberlains, blue orderlies, footmen in gold and green, under the gold and crimson hangings of Salle du Trône, Salon d'Apollon, Salon du Premier Consul, Salon des Maréchaux.

Nazi membership promised to sidestep the laborious, methodical promotion within tedious banks, unheroic department-stores, a defeated army. It supplied a swifter, more purposeful drive towards status. Authority, decked with black shirt, brown shirt, with prospects of a handshake from the Leader, seemed a virile defence against loneliness, private grief, indifference, making one at home in a new, strident, metallic world where all deaths were Siegfried's.

The SS was now arrayed from head to foot in black—black cap with black chinstrap and silver death's head, black tunic over a brown shirt with black leather buttons and black tie, black Sam Browne belt, black breeches and black jackboots. The design of this uniform had left no stone unturned to tickle the imagination of the hierarchically-minded Germans, introducing all sorts of mysterious marks and badges.

Höhne, *The Order of the Death's Head*

Distributed amongst SS grades was a direct appeal to archaism: oak leaves, stars, silver

Kaiser Wilhelm II in Posen 1913. The Kaiser was infatuated with uniforms and parades until 1914, when they had to be turned to practical use. After 1918 he never again wore uniform, nor was asked to.

threads, diamonds, aluminium chevrons.

One evening, at a reception for sober-minded business men, Goering had startled the company by appearing in shorts of gold leather, a toga, sandals revealing toe-nails painted red, an emerald here and there, a large diamond on the hilt of his sword and accompanied by his pet, a lion. His face was made up with brown paste and there was blue cream on his eye-lids.

Lalli Horstmann, *Too Deep for Tears*

flung open and the Grand Master would announce the Emperor; he would make the round of the circle addressing a few questions in Italian to each in turn. Ungainly and unkempt, these women would either gape in panic silence or giggle with panic volubility. Even Napoleon, who had small sense of incongruity, realised in the end that these court ceremonies were misplaced.

Harold Nicolson, *The Congress of Vienna*

Nazis and Fascists presented massed geometrical pageants under towering columns and arches; huge parades and rallies, flowing standards, pounding drums; the ruthless hypnotic tread of uniformed marchers stirring up frenzied intoxications: giant allegorical statues, élitist tableaux—the whole trained on the climax of solitary Leader, the ancient god descending, the Roman dictator hailed at his Triumph. Here all ages fused, BC becomes Now, the royal lions of Tiglath Pileser III join the swastika and the golden, laurelled Bonaparte 'N'.

Within their courts the Kings possessed an established style: Hero and Dictator were at their weakest when trying to imitate it. Exiled on tiny Elba, Napoleon I could not forgo the archetypal trappings.

In the first months of his reign upon the island he attempted to create at least the semblance of a court society. The leading citizens of Elba—the notaries and the apothecaries, the managers of the tunny fisheries and the mines—were provided by the tailors of Leghorn with state uniforms of blue embroidered with silver; the sempstresses of Porto Ferrajo were kept busy stitching trains of yellow or violet cloth to evening gowns designed in the more recent Empire fashions. In the Salle des Pyramides the chamberlains whom he had recruited locally would endeavour to marshal these gaping women into a royal circle; the door would be

Communist dictators readily digest the processions, prostrations, the inner hush of absolute authority. Their Revolutions, though claiming scientific and atheistical freedoms, replace sentimentality about God and Throne by sentimentality about State and Leader. The Marxist Rosa Luxemburg's 'doubt everything' is crushed by the fulsome apparatus of power. A statue of Mao stands 150 feet high at Nanchang. Chinese children intone, 'Chairman Mao is dearer to us than our parents.' *The Thoughts of Chairman Mao* is waved as solution to all problems, from Universal Peace to the unblocking of drains. 'In the face of soldiers armed with Mao Tse-Tung's Thought, even God would lower his head and step aside on the road.' (Canton Radio, 30 June 1966). It was adopted in physics by the Vice-Chancellor of Kirin University. 'As a result we were able to find correct ways of solving problems in such complicated natural phenomena as the internal revolution of molecules.'

Stalin had continued the atmosphere not only of Tsardom but of dim, vanished millenia. One of his victims, Osip Mandelshtam, wrote:

He has taken away the air I breathe:

The Assyrian holds my heart in his hand.

His fellow-terrorist, Khrushchev, 1936, used the address befitting some priest-king:

By lifting their hands against Comrade Stalin they lifted their hands against all the best that humanity possesses. For Stalin is Hope; he is expectation: he is the beacon that guides all progressive Mankind.

Himmler and Heydrich in Vienna 1938.

Milovan Djilas, himself a Communist, though now a heretical and courageous critic of the bureaucracy, 'the new class', wrote of Stalin, in *Conversations with Stalin*:

I myself referred many times in discussion to the crystal clarity of his style, the penetration of his logic, and the aptness of his commentaries, as though they were expressions of the most exalted wisdom. But it would not have been difficult for me, even then, to detect that the style of any other author who wrote in the same way was drab, meagre, and an unblended jumble of vulgar journalism and the Bible.

From *Ivan the Terrible* 1944. Authority in Russia, a country of weak frontiers and continuously assaulted by powerful neighbours, for centuries required divine associations.

Part II Hierarchy in Society

And kings prevented from their proper
  ends
Make a deep gap in men's imagining;
Heroes are nothing without worshipping…
                              Elizabeth Jennings

Morality and ideas tend to reflect social
facts—certain codes of hospitality and
manners depend on the prevalence of servants. Children reared in communities—the
kibbutz, the boarding school—often lack a
pronounced 'Oedipus complex'. Malinowski

Below
From *The Great Dictator* 1940. Charlie Chaplin and
Jack Oakie as Hitler and Mussolini.

Opposite
From *Ivan the Terrible* 1944. The Tsar seems to be
dying. The more enduring power of the Church
remains unquestioned.

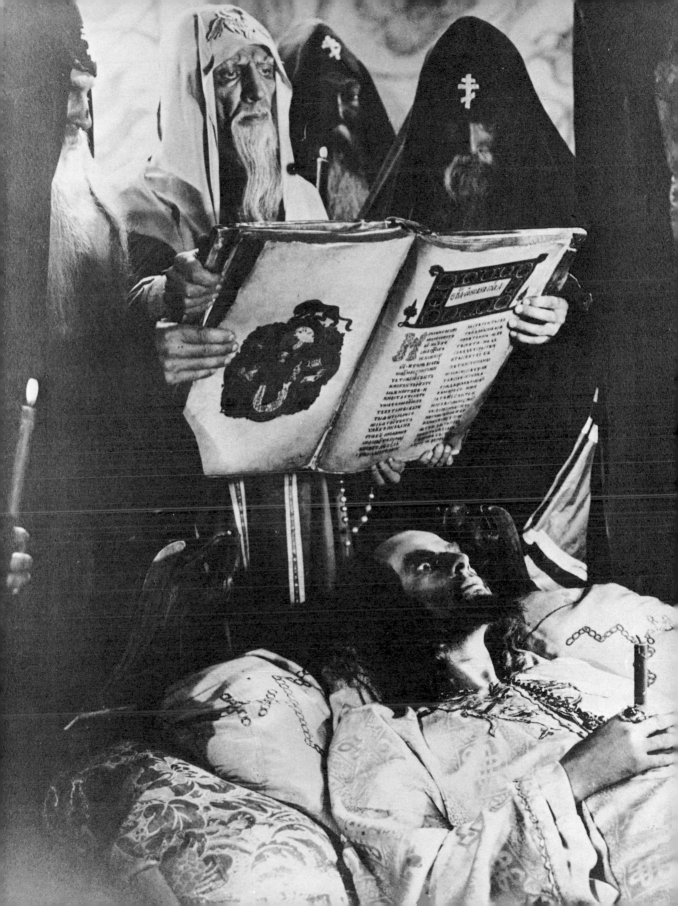

found the 'permissive' Trobrianders clean, healthy, spontaneous, friendly: nearby, the authoritarian Amphlett islanders aggressive, neurotic, servile. Most societies, however, have clear-cut divisions of power, their Heavens envisaged as monarchies or triumvirates, with patriarchal Holy Families. Temptations both to surrender abjectly to the Father, and to overthrow him, lurk in the psyche, though eras occur when the Mother—Goddess, Virgin, Priestess—is dominant, weakening before God, King, Hero, Dictator, but always persisting, as Mariolatry, witchcraft, backstairs intrigue, Women's Liberation.

The most documented ages are of masculine power, expressed by male symbols: pyramids, columns, straight roads, warships, triumphal arches, swords. Julius Caesar was 'Father of his Country'. He and his successors were Pontifex Maximus, uniting spiritual and temporal powers. God the Father presided over Christendom, tolerating no Court of Appeal. Medieval bishops disagreed about whether women had souls. The Council of Trent, 1545, debated whether women were actually human. The Church has always remained patriarchal. 'No man', Jesus had said, 'cometh to the Father save by me.'

From *Alexander Nevsky* 1938. The Teutonic Knights pray, on the eve of their last, fatal battle on the ice, against Alexander, prince and saint.

The Tsar was 'Little Father', Kemal, 'Father of the Turks'. In German families the father was particularly powerful. In more genial England, when Charles II remarked that he was Father of his people, a courtier replied that was certainly father of a great many of them.

The symbolism of power is fluid, even if power itself is less so. The strong admire God's strength, the weak clutch at his promise of retribution. 'He will scatter the proud in the imagination of their hearts.' That orthodoxy assists social unity is appreciated by rulers. 'Society cannot exist without inequality of wealth, and inequality of wealth cannot exist without religion.' (Napoleon I) It can be useful for intellectuals. 'I want my lawyer, my tailor, my servants, even my wife, to believe in God, because then, I think, I shall be cuckolded less often.' (Voltaire)

The god Serapis, conjunction of Apis and Osiris, was fabricated by a Ptolemaic ruler to unite his Egyptian and Syrian subjects. Early Pharaohs ascended to the sky after death, everyone else dwindled into the underworld. Monarchy eventually loses its nerve but conforms even more closely to the primitive pattern: the last Tsar had mystical, fatalistic moods in which, perhaps like the condemned Louis XVI, he saw himself as the Father, to be sacrificed for the Family, the nation. Prince Sihanouk presented himself as the traditional god-ruler, of miraculous birth and divine sanction.

Twentieth-century totalitarian parties share with Christianity its hierarchical order: dead messiah, infallible hero appealing to sacred texts, intolerance—'He that is not with me is against me'—the fellowship of saints and the noble army of Martyrs: spiritual élite, the Elect, subordinating the family to the disciple, and leaving the dead to bury their dead. Also the dogmatic assertion of absolute truth, without proof: ecclesiastical or party tribunals independent of legality: periodic Show Trials of heretics, unbelievers, apostates: apocalyptic Vision of the Perfect Future. An obsession with the past—with Golden Age, Rome, Founding Fathers, medieval Emperors, is simultaneously balanced by desire to abolish it, to sentence it to death as another guilty victim. The Past, which created the hierarchy, sacrificed to the Future, which will disband it. Christianity created BC/AD, as if it had transformed human nature. The French republicans renamed the months, established a ten-day week, and made 1793 Year One of the new dispensation. An Austrian pre-Nazi, Georg von Schonerer, invented a German Year One, AD 9, when 'Germania' defeated Rome in the Teutoburg Forest. Hitler, 'I have to liberate the world from its historic past,' both emphasized the historical heroic continuity of the 'Third Reich', and postulated an unprecedented 'New Order', enthroning his Idea for ever, owing nothing to the past, everything to himself.

Dictators in the Classical World

The strongest poison ever known
Came from Caesar's laurelled Crown.
Blake

No discussion, only Obedience.
Mussolini

A man in the position
Of the Emperor Domitian
Should think twice
Before becoming a Monster of Vice.
E. C. Bentley

As against hereditary kings and monocrats the earliest European Dictators were sixth-century Roman 'Saviours of Society', allowed temporary but absolute powers to defend the Republic. Such was Cincinnatus (*c.* 519–439), summoned against the Aequians, retiring victorious to his farm after three weeks.

Dictatorship has never lost this emergency function. Caesar set himself to repair decades of civil war: Boris Godunov to replace the weak, perhaps half-witted Fedor I: Cromwell to restore a bad military and political situation. There has been talk of Eden behaving like a dictator in the 1956 Suez crisis. Military and political incoherence beckoned Lenin (1917), Riza Shah of Persia (1921), Kemal (1918). The Bonapartes, Mao, hero of epic march and campaign, Castro were acclaimed as overthrowers of cruelty, corruption, profiteering, privilege, inefficiency and foreigners: Franco as retriever of privilege and social discipline. Loss of national morale evokes the providential hero: Kemal, Pilsudski, Horthy, Petain, Mussolini, Hitler, and the military hero, Tito. Redeemer Nkrumah represented anti-imperialist national racialism. Victor Emmanuel I was elected dictator by Italian nationalists against 'the Austrian Tyrant'. White Russian generals established local dictatorships against the Bolsheviks (1919–21). The poet D'Annunzio held Fiume as dictator for a few months (1919). Poverty and backwardness breed a Peron, a Porfirio Diaz. Internal dissensions and party hatred may demand arbitrary solutions from a Solon, Pilsudski, De Gaulle. In 1930, Argentina, Brazil, Peru, Chile, Bolivia all suffered dictatorial coups. Oswald Mosley was forced into untenable Blackshirt extremism largely by the timid ineptitude of his constitutional colleagues and opponents.

Danton, Garibaldi, Enver Pasha, Ludendorff, Churchill, De Gaulle, never quite dictators, fulfilled many dictatorial roles. None would have reached power save for crisis. De Gaulle emerged twice and twice retired, maintaining that his work was unfinished. Churchill exemplifies the origins and limitations of the classical dictator:

At the same time I assumed the office of Minister of Defence, without, however, attempting to define its scope and powers. Thus then, on the night of the tenth of May (1940), at the outset of this mighty battle, I acquired the chief power of the State, which henceforth I wielded in ever-growing measure for five years and three months of world-war, at the end of which time, all our enemies having surrendered unconditionally or being about to do so, I was immediately dismissed by the British electorate from all further conduct of their affairs.
The Gathering Storm

The Roman dictatorship might later extend to political crises, as it had in Athens under

Goya *Colossus*

Josephine Crickmay *Alexander the Great* 1971
drawing from an ancient picture.

Solon (*c.* 638–*c.* 558 BC) and even to
arranging elections or Games in turbulent
times. After 150 years of disuse it revived,
with significant change, Sulla holding it for
three years during violence and class-
convulsions, and Caesar being granted it
for life.

Power is not only a responsibility, it is a
sensual appetite, fully articulated by
Alexander the Great, hereditary King of
Macedon (356–323 BC). His career, as
world-conqueror and god, seemed the climax
of masculine endeavour. An existentialist
without knowing it, he was what Bernard
Shaw said of himself: 'Things have not
happened to me; on the contrary, it is I who
have happened to them.' Unlike many
Romans, totally unlike Napoleon I, Hitler,
Stalin, he respected the conquered and,
as a pupil of Aristotle, was curious about the
nature of people and things. He acknow-
ledged Greek, Persian and Egyptian aristocratic culture as superior to Macedonian,
desiring cosmopolitan unity rather than
narrow hegemony, an example lost on his
twentieth-century successors, contemporary
but less modern. He abolished the prostra-
tion due to monarchs he supplanted. Unrolling vast cultural and political vistas he
died with real problems barely begun, and
his history was swiftly dissolved into his
myth.

Alexander's mother had soaked him with
convictions of his divine origins. Master of
psychological warfare, he had himself proclaimed Son of Zeus, 'a present deity', and,
though no megalomaniac, may have half-
believed it. Whatever the truth, he remained
for centuries locked in divinity.

With ravish'd ears
The monarch hears,
Assumes the god,
Affects to nod
And seems to shake the spheres
                    Dryden, *Alexander's Feast*

It is said that, generations later, a painted
'Alexander' would ride before invaders, to
achieve surrender without fighting. As
'Iskander' he entered Asiatic folk-lore. For
medieval Europe he symbolized heroic and
intellectual adventure, exploring depths of
sky and ocean in magic ships. Napoleon I
kept in his bedroom Altdorfer's *Alexander
Defeating Darius*. His cutting of the Gordian
Knot provided an incisive and lasting image
of direct action, to mislead future power-
addicts.

In the mythology of power, Alexander had
a successor even more inescapable, in whom
two stages of dictatorship, 'Emergency
Saviour' and 'God-Emperor' prophetically
merged.

Civil war, corruption, slave revolts, party

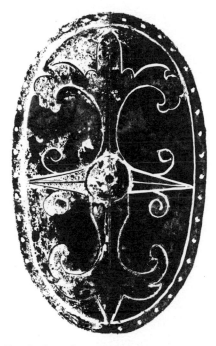

Josephine Crickmay *Roman Shield* 1971

feuds of the later Roman Republic forced the Senate to surrender to dictatorship of army commanders, 'emperors'. Julius Caesar (102–44 BC) rose in the wake of Pompey's conquest of the Near East, and of his own victories in Gaul and Germania. Bloody 'social wars', between Sulla and Marius, had already designed the proscription, massacre, amorality that imperial Italy seldom wholly lost. Caesar himself, at first one of an all-powerful triumvirate with Pompey and the millionaire Crassus, won over the underprivileged radicals against the conservative Senate, as did his spiritual successors, the two Bonapartes. Like Cromwell and Napoleon I he cultivated adroit personal relations with his troops. In the crisis following the triumvirate's dissolution he violated republican legality by marching an army into Rome (49 BC), ostensibly as protection against patrician enemies, headed by Pompey. Progressively stimulated by military success and large-scale organization, he had increasing contempt for constitu-

tional obstructions. Against Pompey he gained dictatorship for eleven days (48 BC), then, as victor, for one year, together with the consulship for five. Though, like John of Leyden, Cromwell, Robespierre, Lenin, Trotsky, no proletarian, he still relied upon 'the People' against the rich and stolid.

With final conquest of the Pompeians he was awarded dictatorship for ten years. He set about enlarging the Empire, reforming law, administration, politics, the calendar, in interests of efficiency, social balance, ex-servicemen. Before his murder he was planning schools, libraries, swifter communications, canals, and the draining of the malarial Pontine Marshes, which Mussolini completed. His ghost, extant in *Tsar* and *Kaiser*, haunted Europe for two thousand years.

Though huge personal debts inspired some of his early power-hunger, Caesar was probably impatient of waste: waste of human potential, resources, lives, by greedy incompetent place-seekers, frauds, time-servers and criminals. A great captain without the handicap of formal military education, cultured and sophisticated, he despised blood-lust and gross revengefulness. Vain and unscrupulous, at times coldly cruel, for tactics, not pleasure, he was also capable of irony, magnanimity, tolerance. He wept for the murdered Pompey. Like De Gaulle he was a capable writer: like Napoleon III he had charm without pomposity. He could be long-suffering, but ruthlessly fixed the limits. This is a reminder that dictators are not always stupid and loutish butchers, and that a Brutus or a Cassius can be a long-winded prig, heir of noble standards which he has neither skill nor imagination to renovate. Poets, perhaps unfairly, usually distrusted him, though he reappears in Shaw's *Caesar and Cleopatra*.

Oh, this military life! this tedious brutal life of action! That is the worst of us Romans: we are mere doers and drudgers: a swarm of bees turned into men. Give me a good talker—one with wit and imagination enough to live without continually doing something.

41

His own Caesar seems to have over-excited Shaw himself who, disenchanted by parliaments and political parties, came fulsomely to praise Stalin and Mussolini, on unsatisfactory hearsay.

We do not know, but can guess, how Caesar considered his role as Pontifex Maximus, guardian of divination, High Priest of Jupiter, and of the temples built to him, though one of his statues, inscribed 'To the Invincible God', was ordained throughout Italy, and his birth-month, Quintilis, renamed Julius.

For centuries thereafter, Roman emperors were deified. One remembers the mad, eccentric or vicious, morbid victims of their own childhood, more eagerly than Augustus, Hadrian, Trajan, as one remembers Duvalier, or Huerta of Mexico. The Western

From *Ivan the Terrible* 1944. The tyranny of the Tsar throws a huge shadow, extending long after the collapse of the Romanovs.

Empire endured far longer than any subsequent international order. That in Constantinople collapsed only in 1453, its spiritual prerogatives claimed by Moscow, 'the Third Rome', protector of the Orthodox Faith, and Holy Places, within and without Russia. Thus Ivan the Terrible, Peter the Great, Catherine the Great, Stalin, were, in a sense, 'Roman Emperors', their imperialism sanctified by a sense of Russian Mission strong since Mongol times, that so attracted Dostoievsky, and intellectuals nearer home. Charlemagne (742–814) saw himself as restoring the Western Empire: 'Holy Roman Emperors' ruled in Vienna until 1804.

> The Roman Empire prospered under the Principate when it was administered as a commonwealth of still autonomous but no longer sovereign states; it decayed with the decay of local autonomy and with the transformation of the world government from an instrument for keeping the peace into an agency for the centralised bureaucratic administration of local as well as common affairs. The history of the Chinese empire tells the same tale.
>
> Arnold Toynbee, *Acquaintances*

The Empire bequeathed rival political ideals: imperialist, aristocratic, republican, even democratic. Considerations not only of conquest and exploitation, but of the proper uses of government, leisure, life itself. Eighteenth-century gentlemen collected busts of Cato, quoted Cicero in Parliament, held stoic morality of self-reliance and moral world-order, Roman sense of power tinged not only with privilege but responsibility. German communists (1920) and a more recent British movement invoked the Roman slave-leader, Spartacus.

> From the pits then open laid,
> Breath of Legions upward rolled,
> Women, boys in cavalcade,
> Here their clay, their ore, their gold!
> See the host on mountain ridge—
> Cohorts tread in rhythms regal!
> For the Caesar's scion's eagle
> Wide the portal and the bridge.
>
> Stefan George (1868–1933)

Reviving in the Middle Ages, save in Britain, Roman Law was authoritarian, enabling a Charlemagne, a Napoleon, to decide, even invent laws. They never allowed a legal opposition. Roman institutions ever obsessed violent and ambitious men. The Roman plebiscite was used by the Jacobins to confirm territorial thefts, by the Bonapartes and De Gaulle to evade parliamentary blockades and red tape, confirm their régimes and divide the opposition. Soviet one-party elections are miniature plebiscites. Napoleon I took power as 'First Consul' after a plebiscite, then, like Caesar, Consul for life, finally Emperor. He had his Roman regimental 'eagles', which also dominated the crests of Romanovs, Habsburgs, Hohenzollerns. Louis Napoleon, attempting a coup (1839), lacking an eagle, paraded instead a caged vulture. Attacking Fiume, D'Annunzio, who first used the 'Hitler' salute, waving Roman rhetoric like a banner, adorned his troops with cocks' feathers when eagles' were used up. Napoleon I, Mazzini, Mussolini, appealing for Italian unity, evoked the splendours of the lost Empire. Mussolini deliberately imitated Rome when organizing the Fascist militia, with consuls, centurions, legions, fasces, pledging himself to a revived Roman Empire, of heroic force.

> War alone brings to its highest tension all human energy and puts the stamp of nobility upon those nations who have the courage to face it. All other tests are substitutes, which never really place men in the position where they are forced to make the great choice—the alternative of life and death.

Hitler too spoke of 'the stupendous impression produced on me by the War—the greatest of all impressions. For that, individual interest—the interest of one's own ego—could be subordinated to the common interest, that the great heroic struggle of our people demonstrated in overwhelming fashion.' (1922)

The Italianate Bonapartes rebuilt Paris in imperial Roman style, tall grandeur and straight lines, cowing the people, facilitating

the movement of eye and of troops. Personal Power uses architecture more to stagger the mind than provide homes: monuments immortalize the ruler. Shih Hwang Ti's Great Wall, the Great Pyramid, Soekarno's huge stadiums, the gigantic Assyrian bas-reliefs, Peter the Great's St Petersburg were eternity-symbols, stone rhetoric, conquering Time and Death.

The history of power is tinctured by Rome's bloodstream. The Triumph may still be the dream of young Red Guard, neo-Fascist legionary, average politician, small-town voter. The banners, drums, trumpets, loot, ovations, prisoners, inescapable posters.

A huge painting, sumptuously framed represented the Subjugation of Marseilles. There followed statues of the Rhine, the Rhone and the Ocean in chains, carved out of pure gold to signify Caesar's expedition against Britain. After the statues came the white bulls with gilded horns destined for the sacrifice followed by Vercingetorix at the head of a group of Gallic chieftains. Seventy-two lictors, an unprecedented number, escorted Caesar, who wore a purple toga and a laurel wreath. He carried a branch of laurel in one hand and a sceptre in the other, and his face was painted the colour of blood. He showed no emotion. Expressionless, staring straight ahead, he seemed to be rapt in the contemplation of his own divinity; and he seems not to have heard the scurrilous songs sung by the mobs lining the streets, by the soldiers who marched behind him and by the actors who ran beside his chariot and fearlessly taunted him.

Robert Payne, *The Roman Triumph*

The Emperor Trajan AD 98–117

Napoleon Bonaparte as the Liberator of Italy 1797. The French revolutionary era loved to identify itself with Republican Rome: heroic, simple, liberating, stern.

To medievals, 'Progress' meant not futurism and a democratic unknown but a return to Rome or Primitive Christianity, glowing poles of life. Through design or frustration, most revolutionary movements have been authoritarian, their leaders apt to become 'Roman Emperors', reserving the State for dynasty, Party, adopted favourite.

'Again, recall the alternatives. Either Providence or Atoms,' had advised Emperor Marcus Aurelius (121–180), but classical philosophers had long ceased to speculate atomically, analytically. Scientific experiment degenerated into scientific speculation, akin to music and rhetoric. Plato and Aristotle obstructed medieval scientific and political development, either through mistranslation or by being translated only too well. Aristotle believed in inferior races and classes, fit only for slavery. Plato envisaged ideal solutions and perfect shapes, excluding the irregular, independent, eccentric and poetic. Theorists, maintained Spengler, himself a theorist, kill revolutions: Plato, called in to reform Syracuse, created only muddle. The high-minded Platonists, Robespierre and Saint-Just, the Russian Old Bolshevik intellectuals, Trotsky, Bukharin, Zinoviev, with too much reading, 'Highbrow hocus-pocus . . . Let's pretend', and too little psychology, delivered their country to imperialisms denied by every promise they had ever made.

Plato had demanded that 'no man, woman or child should ever be without an officer set over him, and that none should ever get into the habit, even in his private thoughts, of acting on his own initiative, either seriously or in fun.' (*The Laws*) Like too many thinkers without responsibility, he thought in capital letters. A totalitarian élite must use the State to promote Truth, Beauty, Justice, Virtue, securing control of all children. Thomas More's *Utopia* envisaged a society of fifty-four identical towns, citizens wearing standardized clothes, living communal lives,

Pieter Bruegel *Big Fish Eat Little Fish* 1556

Albrecht Dürer *The Resurrection*

all retiring at 8 p.m., devoted to Higher Education, with two years compulsory farming, a stipulation that would have delighted Himmler. Such ideas, reinforced by Spartan and Republican heroics, enthralled the young French Revolutionaries who saw themselves as Brutus and Cassius trying to persuade the horrible; the most extremist of them all, Baboeuf, called himself 'Gracchus'. The world, cried Saint-Just, has been empty since the Romans.

The Jacobins had drastic schemes for imposing discipline, public spirit, goodness, by Law, finally by Terror, subordinating all to the State, 'for the larger good'. Robespierre, Cato of the Revolution, ordained, 'There must be one will, and one will only.' Saint-Just, Lycurgus the Lawgiver, envisaged 'Institutions' to transform France to the Platonist State. 'Procreation is obligatory: spouses childless after seven years of union or who fail to adopt, must be separated by law and leave each other.' 'Murderers will be dressed in black all their lives, and killed if they abandon it. Whoever has lived innocently will, at sixty, wear a white scarf.' Children were to be taken to State schools at five: at fifteen to State farms and barracks. Friendless citizens were to be banished, everyone declaring annually his friends' names 'in the public temple'.

Philosophers, artists, intellectuals, as much part of political dynamics as the politicians, are often, in temperament, profoundly undemocratic. D. H. Lawrence wrote to Bertrand Russell: 'I don't believe in democratic control . . . the working man shall elect superiors for the things that concern him immediately, no more. From the other classes, as they rise, shall be selected the higher governors. The thing must culminate in one real head, as every organic thing must —no foolish republics with foolish presidents, but an elected king, something like Julius Caesar.'

Christianity effected changes of allegiance more swiftly than changes of heart. King Clovis accepted baptism, then slaughtered his family. Human thought was not drained of ancient pictures. Personifying unchanged human impulses, the gods remained, old friends on half-pay, sometimes disguised as saints. Emperor Alexander Severus (205–35) retained images of Abraham, Orpheus, Christ. The seventh-century King Raedwald of East Anglia had altars both to Christ and Woden. Ivory panels of the Vatican's ninth-century Throne of St Peter are adorned with mythological and zodiacal symbols. Weapons, tournaments, ikons, prayers, had long links with magic and blood-sacrifice.

Jesus himself was captured by the old gods. Gospels and legends did not outline a character full and consistent, so that changing fortunes elicited different natures from Christ: Good Shepherd, Avenging Judge, sharp-tongued *sans-culotte*, Meek Victim, pre-Raphaelite poet, Puritan moralist, beardless Comrade, or bearded in the image of Byzantine Autocrat in Splendour: motionless, staring, inhuman: a further Caesar.

Militants howl absolute values and premises, but Time fluctuates, progress is relative, chronology misleads. Each age has its personality and counter-personality, its code and emblems, its seeds, not only of decline but of rebirth. A conservative figure is not always damnable. When Count Witte proposed to the anti-Semitic Tsar Alexander III (1845–94) the deportation and drowning of Jews in the Black Sea, the Tsar replied that he was uninterested in obscene jokes and requested Witte to withdraw. Hitler's response is more predictable.

Pre-Revolutionary Totalitarian Tendencies

The Holy Catholic Church is Single and Apostolic: that is a Dogma which Faith enjoins us to believe and to maintain: outside the Church there is neither Salvation nor Forgiveness of Sins.

Pope Boniface VIII, 1302

Why these murders and horrors? It would be shown that War is a business, divine in itself, and as needful and necessary to the world as eating and drinking or any other work.

Martin Luther

We want to educate the citizens of the State so that they shall be incapable of willing anything other than what the State ordains them to will.

J. G. Fichte

Modern Dictators only pushed to the limit the traditional power-politics of Throne and Altar, Castle and Cathedral. Both Church and State, though inherently conservative, contain radical elements and, like individuals, abound with contradictions. Both are concerned not only with suppressing but exploiting human energies. 'Jesus and No Quarter' was a seventeenth-century Presbyterian war-cry. 'Jesus' appeared in Mau-Mau oaths. 'Bolsheviks should not hesitate to use barbarous methods to combat barbarism.' (Lenin) Timoleon of Syracuse (d. 337 BC), benevolent and wise, murdered his intolerable brother for the public good, as did Catherine the Great her husband. The God-approved killing of King Eglon, by Ehud, gave one biblical sanction for 'moral' murder.

The third-century Chinese 'Legalists' held that the People functioned to supply food and warrior for the State, which existed for war. The Spartans, who talked peace while organizing for war, postulated a master-race supported by slaves, a situation periodically threatened by reformer-kings. Rome enslaved and destroyed, while dispensing law and order. The Emperors had secret police, sometimes killed off senators.

The Holy Roman Emperor, Frederick II, 'Wonder of the World' (1194–1250), poet, ornithologist, law-giver, supreme ruler, lit up the European imagination as thoroughly as Alexander, Caesar Imperator, Charlemagne, names clashing like shields. His Sicilian kingdom was centred on himself; he has been called Hegel's God on Earth. The powerful and mysterious Philip the Fair (1285–1314), virtual founder of the French State, violated safe-conducts, humiliated the Papacy, coldly engineered the expropriation and judicial murders of the Templars, in a frame-up Stalinist in its conception and scope.

Neither monarch, gifted, unscrupulous, modern, had any more democracy or Christian love than did the eighteenth-century 'Reforming Despots', Peter, Catherine, Frederick the Great, Joseph II. 'Everything *for* the people, nothing *by* the people.' (Frederick) Catherine advised the Governor of Moscow, 'The day when our peasants wish to become enlightened, both you and I will lose our jobs.' All desired efficient, disciplined States pivoted on royal ascendancy, none ducked war. 'I love war because of the glory it brings,' Frederick admitted; though glory, it has been observed, is only the sum of the dead. 'Ambition, self-interest, and the desire to make people talk of me carried the day, and I decided for war.' Frederick's confession should not be overlooked by pacifist academics, nor Colonel Peard, an English volunteer for Garibaldi: 'I have great respect for Italian independence, but I am also very fond of shooting.'

He kept a pocket-book in which to log his victims.

No monarch, even few nineteenth-century Liberals and humanitarians, would have queried Mussolini's belief in 'the fertilizing, beneficent and unassailable inequality of man'. Though involuntarily preparing revolution and dictatorship, the kings were seldom themselves dictators, having neither emergency function nor the need to challenge the gods in order to become gods. They were monocrats, engaged less in their mission than their office. Having inherited power,

Fred Uhlman *Jugglers*. From Uhlman's *Captivity* (publ. 1946). Fred Uhlman was once a distinguished anti-Nazi lawyer. After a courageous public fight against the regime he left Germany, first for Paris, then Britain, for a distinguished career as artist and writer. His drawings here (see also pages 53, 56, 99) were done during internment on the Isle of Man 1939–40.

Lucas Cranach the Younger *Luther Preaching*, c. 1540

they wished to use it to maximum effect for everyone, not least for themselves. The dictators had to be more in a hurry, to galvanize nature, to re-charge or abolish traditional institutions. Since they had inherited nothing they had to create everything, at whatever cost.

Church and State needed to control human passions more than to induce moral grandeur by exalted example. The contrast between discipline and goodness was necessarily more notable in the Church.

Christian teaching was as contradictory as Tolstoy, or Bernard Shaw, whom Chesterton compared to a tree with its roots in the air. Jesus had said, 'This is my commandment, that you love one another as I have loved you.' Yet, though tender to the adulteress, he threatened dissenters with the outer darkness, the furnace, the wailing and gnashing of teeth, and cursed a fig-tree for not blossoming out of season. Augustine taught, 'Love whole-heartedly, then do what you like,' but also, 'that the saints may enjoy their beatitude more fully, a perfect sight is granted them of the punishment of the damned.' The preservation of sacred texts can be a questionable asset.

Lucas Cranach the Elder *The Difference Between Christ and Antichrist, c.* 1545

'Fanaticism', said the Jacobin fanatic, Saint-Just, 'is the work of European priest-craft.' Charlemagne and his bishops Christianized Germans in bloody wars. Christ's 'Compel them to come in' was accepted too literally, reappearing in Robespierre's wish 'to compel people to be free'. Guthrum imposed Christianity on his Vikings after defeat by Alfred the Great. Harald of Denmark and the ruffianly St Vladimir of Russia accepted it as a clause in military and commercial treaties: Olaf of Norway because he preferred it: Lithuanians, 1386, were forcibly converted when their ruler married a Catholic.

Christianity itself was shackled to too much past, particularly to biblical apartheid: Chosen and Gentile, Elect and Damned. Joshua reduced Gideonites to hewers of wood and drawers of water, fulfilling God's promise to Moses, 'I will deliver the people of the land into your hand, and thou shalt drive them out before thee.'

Much of this was incorporated by Christianity, seldom a religion of geniality and tolerance, with priests still apt not only to reject the rights of other religions but those of women. Europe always deplored Disraeli's view that all sensible men are of the same religion. Jesus, for once, had spoken unambiguously, 'He that is not with me is against me,' as had Jehovah, 'Thou shalt have no other gods but me.' All this justified violence and persecutions barely credible save to an age that knew Stalin and Hitler. Holy Wars for Holy Truths and Holy Places—'powers of the first rank' (Spengler) —bred each other unendingly. The Norman Conquest, even John of Gaunt's expedition for the Portuguese crown, were awarded Papal Certificates as 'crusades'. Franco designated his civil war a crusade (1947). Cardinal Spellman (December 1966) declared the Americans in Vietnam were 'defending the cause of God'.

Henry V invaded France under 'God's

Will', as Hitler justified his Terror as the Will of Race and History. 'Wars', enjoined Pope Gregory the Great, 'are to be sought, for the sake of spreading the republic in which we perceive God to be revered.' This recalls Baden-Powell, Boer War hero, and Chief Scout:

> You have all heard of the bravery of the Japs in their War against Russia, how they feared nothing and willingly went to their death in order that their country might win. This spirit of sacrificing themselves is called Bushido, and is just the spirit which every fellow must have if he means to be a real true Scout.
>
> *Yarns for Scouts*

Nineteenth-century Zulu braves had to 'blood their spears'. Similarly the Czech Taborites, scolders of Private Property, held that every believer 'should wash his hands in the blood of Christ's foes', and for Mao, 'Communism is not love but a weapon for hammering the enemy.' For Fichte, 'No Law or Right exists between States save the right of the stronger. A people metaphysically predestined has the moral right to complete its destiny with all the means of power and sagacity.' 'Kill them all, God will recognize his own', Innocent III's Legate allegedly said at the massacre of Béziers (1209), during a crusade against the morally superior Albigensians. This is the ethic not only of Béziers but Hiroshima.

Fred Uhlman *The Militants* 1939–40 from *Captivity*

The contest between Elect and Damned implied a determinism as strict as that of Darwin, Marx, Freud, Hitler, surviving the Enlightenment and strengthened by the Revolution. Augustine's Predestination was opposed by the Celtic Pelagius, as Freud was by Sartre, the Pelagian Caelestus declaring that it is the easiest thing in the world to change our will by an act of will. This is eagerly grasped by political zealots indignant at Man conceived as helpless victim of God, Sin, Nature, the Unconscious or even historical inevitability, though, if disillusioned, they may assuage their resentment by Terror.

Augustine's belief 'A man is living badly and perhaps in the predestination of God he he is Light; another lives well, and perhaps he is as black as night', relieved authority from the onus of individual morality. Pope Sixtus IV was involved in a murder plot against Lorenzo the Magnificent and his brother (who actually was killed), to be stabbed by two priests at the elevation of the Host.

To Christianity, none appeared more liable to damnation than the Jew, that enduring rival, ambiguous through having both bred Jesus and killed him. Philip Augustus, St Louis, the atheist Frederick II, Luther, Voltaire, Goethe, were in varying degrees, anti-semitic, as were Dostoievsky, Wagner, Belloc, Chesterton, Ezra Pound, T. S. Eliot, Marx, Nicholas II, Stalin. Norman Cohn relates that the medical faculty of Vienna University, 1610, 'solemnly announced that Jewish physicians were obliged by their laws to poison every tenth Christian patient'. Extremists pound relentlessly on man's primitive fear of secret societies, rumours of mysterious ritual and Black Magic.

The Jew, like Devil and Moslem, was also a scapegoat for what otherwise would be blamed on God, feeble clerical magic and spiritual diplomacy, or administrative malpractice. Dictators likewise justify purges, invasions, repression, by blaming Trotsky, counter-revolutions, Freemasons, Jews.

Medieval Jews were popularly associated with satanism, ritual murder, plague dissemination. The clerical Council of Arles (1235) ordered them to wear yellow patches. Racial purity was propagated in Spain against Jew and Moslem, ending in the expulsion of both (1492). Through Papal Bulls, 1414 and 1418, the University of St Bartholomew, Salammanco, introduced racial discrimination, and Spanish racialism was legal until 1865.

Pope Innocent III (1160–1216) addressed the Count of Nevers: 'The Jews, like the fratricidal Cain, are doomed to wander about the earth as fugitives and vagabonds, and their faces must be covered with shame. They are under no circumstances to be protected by Christian princes but, on the contrary, to be condemned to serfdom.'

This was slow to modify. Supported by Nicholas II, Orthodox priests assisted the Black Hundreds, terrorists advocating unlimited autocracy and the deportation or extermination of Jews. Karl Lueger's Austrian anti-semitic Christian Social Party attracted the young Hitler. Appealing to world Catholicism against the Red Army (1920) Polish bishops referred to 'the race which has the leadership of Bolshevism in its hands, has already in the past subjugated the whole world through gold and banks, and now, driven by the everlasting imperialist greed that flows in its veins, is already aiming at the subjugation of the nations.' The Nazi paper, *Der Sturmer*, still reporting Jewish ritual murders, announced (1936) that 'whoever vanquishes World Jewry will save Earth from the Devil'. Hitler himself claimed, 'In resisting the Jew I am fighting the Lord's Battle.'

Christianity has always contained those to succour Jewry, the poor, the enslaved. Despite a reputation for casuistry, and an authoritarian organization on which Himmler modelled much of the SS, also admiring Loyola's meditational exercises, the Jesuits, progressive in physics and mathematics, were anti-racialist, ruling compassionately in Canada and Paraguay until recalled by the Pope, while their co-religionists slaughtered several million

Indians in Mexico, Peru and the Carribean. Yet to this day Pope Pius XII is being condemned for never publicly denouncing Nazi atrocities.

State values tarnished the Roman Church's moral pretensions, perhaps permanently. The Index of Forbidden Books attempted to control the intellect. The Inquisition, in eighteenth-century Cadiz alone, confiscated 8000 books in nine years. (Henry Kamen, *Spanish Inquisition*) Particularly in Spain, the Holy Office, anticipating Jacobins, Bolsheviks, Nazis, Maoists, practised torture and brain-washing, encouraged denunciation by friends, neighbours, relatives, servants, children. From the sixteenth century, trials were secret, with witnesses and accusers anonymous. No reasons for arrest were divulged: victims were presumed guilty and had to prove innocence, forced to answer at once, without a lawyer. In 1664 a Mexican penitent, covered with honey and feathers, was made to stand four hours in the sunlight, watching a mass burning. Heretics, Jews, witches suffered in scores. The last European woman thus to be burnt alive was in 1780, 'for carnal knowledge of the Devil'.

Amongst the masses the Inquisition was never as unpopular as might be supposed, and the famous Jacobin Camille Desmoulins praised the Revolutionary Clubs as 'Inquisitorial Tribunals of the People'. Inability of

Goya *The Tribunal of the Inquisition* 1794

revolutionaries to forget such procedures has postponed indefinitely any genuine Revolution in which 'the criminal might blush for his weakness instead of blanching at his condemnation' (Saint-Just)

Totalitarian pressures, nevertheless, are seldom as total as theory insists. Internal power struggles have often emasculated dictatorships. Thus the Inquisition was hated by the Jesuits, occasionally rebuked from Rome. Though quickly forced to recant, on 18 April 1482, Sixtus IV did proclaim that 'for lust for wealth', the Spanish Inquisition had practised 'theft, torture, murder, perjury, and encouraged false witness'. The Jesuit St Francis Borgia had writings on the Index: the late Teilhard de Chardin was denied the *imprimatur*.

'Among God's miracles, some are Articles of Faith, like that of the Virgin Birth—and precisely because the Lord wished them to remain incomprehensible so that faith in them be the more worthy.' (St Thomas Aquinas (1227–74), *Summa Theologia*) This

Fred Uhlman *Child, Balloon and Priest* 1939–40
from *Captivity*

remains the basis of dictatorship, authority loving to engender mystery and exoticism.

Church and State, though rivals for men's obedience, jealous as priest and doctor at a death-bed, were at one on the principle of obedience. The Cathedral was as much an armoury as the Castle. 'This so evident alliance of all the charlatans', Stendhal said, referring to Napoleon's coronation by the Pope.

An appeal to Jesus as Rebel or individualist was dangerous. Though St Francis of Assisi, a forerunner of Albert Schweitzer in 'reverence for life', escaped condemnation for heresy, those who seriously followed his teachings did not. Cardinal Richelieu (1585–1642) considered that France had two diseases, Heresy and Liberty. The Church, as guardian of Absolute Truth, could not accept that heresy, like laughter, can prevent life becoming a ritual of cliché and apathy. Orthodoxy fears the heretic more than the pagan or unbeliever. The extreme Left, Stalinist or Anarchist, hates rival Socialists—Bevin, Masaryk, Tito, Nagy, Dubcek—more than Franco, Vorster, De Gaulle. Celebrating the Golden Jubilee of Chinese Communism, the Maoist *People's Daily*, virtually ignoring 'Western Imperialism', castigated the Russian Communist leaders as 'mad present-day social imperialists and world-storm-troopers, opposing China, opposing communism and opposing the People.' (1 July 1971)

Church and State intellectualism fostered Antinomianism, that certain people are 'above the Law', certain groups are beneath it, like a tiresome opera star reiterating that art excuses bad manners. Pope and Emperor collaborated in burning alive Jan Hus (1415), following a safe-conduct. 'Everything is legal to Virtue in order to conquer Vice.' (Robespierre) 'In politics is no morality, only expediency.' (Lenin) Democracy itself does not automatically recoil from it, though Churchill reluctantly refused to seize the vital Irish ports in 1940 and Sir Richard Allen (*Malaysia: Prospect and Retrospect*) observes that, through legal scruples, the British refused to arrest key communists

and rebels before the long and bloody jungle war (1948).

Stalin betrayed the Lublin Committee after formal guarantees (1946). In 1956, 'the arrest and execution of the Hungarians Nagy and Palmatir by the Russian and Hungarian Communists following a safe-conduct is the anti-communist case in a nutshell.' (Camus)

Stalin's daughter, Svetlana, (*Only One Year*) blamed the dictator's cynicism and shiftiness on his seminary training: its casuistry, dogmatism, deviousness, opportunism. He was convinced that 'the precept

George Grosz *Arrested* 1920

about using any means to attain an end produced far greater results than lofty ideals ever could'. Hitler's architectural and technological expert, Speer, confessed, 'the sight of a man in misery may have stirred my feelings, but it did not influence my actions. As far as feelings were concerned I displayed only sentimentality; where decisions were required, I was guided by the principles of "the means to the end"' (1970). Eichmann, organizer of the SS extermination policy, had strict Presbyterian upbringing. Colonial Puritans from many lands enslave blacks, sometimes as 'Sons of Cain'.

The Reformation was largely unconcerned either with political morality or the rights of women and children. The rival protagonists ignored the internationalism, rational, detached, humane, of More, Erasmus, Montaigne, as it did the stupendous gaiety of Rabelais' 'Drink not simply of wine but of Life and all it has to offer.' Protestants burnt Servetus; Catholics, Bruno, giving point to Voltaire's remark that we have enough religion to hate and persecute, not enough to love and succour.

Exaggerated mistrust in fellow men exaggerates faith in the Big Stick. Luther, like Marx, a spiritual dictator, to whom Reason 'was the arch-whore', was darkly influenced by ferocious German social wars, and ran a dark tongue into the universe. Impulsive human nature, in essence evil, could be checked only by Faith, toil and obedience. War was a rod given to rulers by God. 'The hand that bears the Sword of Government is no longer man's but God's. Not man it is, but God, who hangs, breaks on wheels, beheads, strangles and wages war.' 'Such wondrous times are these, that one Prince can merit heaven better with bloodshed than another with fear.'

Descendent Churches have shown, even to moderate régimes, a subservience surely exorbitant. Cardinal Bourne (30 October 1909) rebuked Conan Doyle and the Congo Reform Association for interfering in the Congo atrocities. Under autocracies, for brute survival, servility, though cowardly, was more defensible. The Tsarist Church became a State Department, absorbed in liturgy and political toadyism rather than morality, protest, charity. 'Disobedience to our Sovereign Tsar is disobedience to God.' Bolshevism changed little. In public prayers the atheist Stalin was 'Leader Elect of God'. The Metropolitan Sergius pronounced (1927), 'We must show not by words that we are faithful citizens of the Soviet Union, loyal to the Government.'

Elsewhere, many honest Christians fatally hesitated before dictators who promised to scourge Reds, Anarchists, Jews, Freemasons, street hooligans. Their leaders were more hasty to render unto Caesar. 'A man sent to us by God,' Pope Pius XI said of Mussolini, whom an Archbishop of Canterbury vouched for as 'the one giant figure in Europe'.

The German Churches, more than the Austrian, who obsequiously welcomed the Nazi theft of their country, courageously helped frustrate the Nazi extermination of the old, sick, deformed and insane: individuals, the Catholic Count Bishop von Galen, the Protestant theologian Bonhoeffer, Pastor Niemöller—like the Dutch Catholic Church—made uncompromising resistance. But the Churches in general were trapped in the aftermath of those to whom the Sermon on the Mount meant moral sluggishness and sycophantic acceptance. As evidence, the following telegrams:

Impressed by the great occasion when the leaders of the German Evangelical Church assembled in company with the Reich Chancellor, they unanimously reaffirm their unconditional loyalty to the Third Reich and its Leader. In the strongest terms possible, the Church leaders condemn all activities of critics of the State, Nation and Party, designed to endanger the Third Reich.

27 January 1934

The Roman Hierarchy (20 August 1935) saluted Hitler:

The Bishops assembled at Fulda for the forthcoming Conference send to the Leader and Chancellor of the German Reich their loyal and respectful greetings

From *Ivan the Terrible* 1944. Artillery, Lewis
Mumford has said, simplified the art of government.

which, according to Divine Command,
we owe to the holder of the State's
supreme office and authority.

Franz Stangl, 'the best Camp Commander
in Poland', commandant of Treblinka Camp,
imprisoned for 400,000 deaths, spoke (*Daily
Telegraph Magazine* 8 October 1971) of the
significant influence of Cardinal Innitzer's
call to Austrian Catholics to cooperate with
Hitler.

Spiritual dictatorships can be as drastic
as knives and scaffolds. William James, in
his *Varieties of Religious Experience*, quotes
Father Rodriguez, confirming a leadership

principle as yet unbroken in the politics of
Church and State. The Jesuit recollected
Ignatius Loyola's saying that were the Holy
Father to order him to sail in the first boat to
be found in Ostia, and let himself sail
without oar, rudder or food, 'he would
gladly obey, not only with alacrity but
without anxiety or repugnance, and even
with a great internal satisfaction.'

To indulge in action or caprice from what
passes as free choice can sometimes be more
momentous than storming a Bastille or
planting a flag at the Pole and, some maintain,
as infrequent.

Dictatorship of the Group

Alison Morgan *The Guillotine Governs (Barère)* 1971

What constitutes a Republic is the absolute destruction of whatever stands in its way.
Saint-Just

I know nothing more beautiful than the Appassionata Sonata and could listen to it every day. It is wonderful, almost superhuman music. It always makes me thrill with warmth and pride that man can produce such wonders. It deeply touches one's nerves. One feels like saying something loving, something silly, and stroking the heads of men, who can live in such purgatory and yet produce such beauty. But to-day we must not stroke people's hair—if we did, our hand would be bitten off. To-day we must bang them on the head—bang them mercilessly, though, as an ideal, we are against any form of force against man. How damnably hard is our task.

Lenin

Camus held that totalitarianism is invariably worse than whatever it seeks to remedy. Its rigours are usually in somewhat harsher proportion to those of the régime it has replaced, the effort to do so necessitating a violence difficult to shed. The French Revolution became more despotic and nationalistic than the Bourbons: the viciousness of the Commune exceeded that of Napoleon III. The frustrations of intellectuals help inspire revolutions and, once in power, a Robespierre, Rigault, Lenin, tend towards the dogmatic, pitiless, humourless.

Minorities, revolting against authority that frequently seems more formidable than it actually is, find exceptional psychic energy, messianic fervour, trust in the overwhelming father-figure of God, Party, Good Old Cause. The afflatus of the Leveller, John Lilburne:

I lifted up my soul to my old and faithful councillor, the Lord Jehovah. He presently came into my soul with a mighty power, and raised me high above myself, and gave me that present resolution that was able to leave me, with a great deal of assured confidence, to grapple with a whole host of men.

That assured confidence sustained a Napoleon, Kemal, Hitler, and inspired an almost overwhelming sixteenth-century fanaticism, Anabaptism.

Levellers opposed the property-owning Cromwellians; Jacobins the wealthy

60

Girondins; Paris Communards the Orthodox Republicans; Bolsheviks the Social Democratic Mensheviks. Luther had denounced the Pope and the abuse of property. German and Dutch Anabaptists, outraged by the hideous class wars and by Luther's retreat from radicalism, denounced Pope and Luther alike, together with all property, all wealth. Church and State were the Devil's deceits, perverting Christ's simple truths: infant baptism was a fraud by which priests kidnapped helpless recruits. Let by charismatic prophets they howled out biblical texts to excuse murder, apartheid, community of goods and land, dictatorship of the self-appointed Elect. They dedicated themselves to purging humanity, first by pacifism and rhetoric, then by violence, of riches, class-distinctions, war, law, evil. At their most spectacular they seized Münster, 1533, expelling all Catholics and Lutherans in the name of the Lord. Stimulated by the prophecies of the barely sane John Matthias, organized by a triumvirate—the demagogic ex-Lutheran preacher, Rottman, a wealthy clothier Knipperdollink, and the young actor-playwright-tailor, John of Leyden— they staged a one-party election and took total power. Their polygamy, justified by Old Testament patriarchs, their collectivism and Terror, resounded throughout conformist, propertied Europe with the shock of Jacobinism and Leninism. John of Leyden proclaimed himself King of the World, a 'Roman Emperor', reigning above twelve dukes. A remarkable showman, he unrolled a perpetual tableau of processions, music, banquets, executions, oratory, though the city was soon besieged by indignant Catholics and Protestants, united for once against the appalling, mocking intruder. John publicly married twelve wives, allegedly killing one with his own hands. Jeering at each of the Ten Commandments, he fully exposed the most secret lusts and ambitions; in his radiance and tyranny was the lure of the forbidden. He enforced absolute obedience with expulsion, mass-killings, apocalyptic threats to Europe. When his cause collapsed in fire and blood, starvation, betrayal, viola-

Heinrich Aldegrever *John of Leyden* 1534–5

tion of safe-conducts, John was executed by a Catholic bishop, on a red-hot throne wearing a scorching crown, afterwards, with his associates, hung in cages from the Cathedral towers. He has never been quite forgotten. Thomas Nashe, Durrenmatt, and Meyerbeer have treated the Anabaptists in plays and the grandest of Grand Opera.

The Anabaptists had been visionary archaists. Jacobins and Bolsheviks wanted not only to purify but modernize society, by strengthening Law and State. Neither was sympathetic to Church, though few French were atheists. Most of the French revolutionaries began as moderate monarchists, fiercely idealistic. 'Wherever the French armies come, all taxes, tithes, and privileges of rank are to be abolished' (The Convention, 15 December 1792). The sacred texts were from Rousseau, with occasional approval for Jesus as the first *sans-culotte*.

The Jacobins, on the Left ('Left' and 'Right' are always said to derive from the Republican seating arrangements—though the left hand has immemorial dynamic associations, often feared) were forced into terroristic republicanism by foreign invasion, civil war, royal treachery, eloquent but weak Girondin ministers. They convulsed the Paris mob by proposing furious final solutions to these, and to corruption, hunger, rising prices. Like the Bolsheviks they grabbed power as a violent minority during a war crisis, hundreds of Jacobin clubs controlling and intimidating public opinion, ignoring the official Moderate government. War and terror had not been of their seeking. 'A civil war could be a great school of public virtue. Peace will set us back . . . we can be regenerated by blood alone.' Thus the revered Girondin Madame Roland, a type of which Burghley might have been thinking —presumably not of his employer—when he said that there is nothing more fulsome than a she-fool.

Mostly very young, of unsettled childhood, working in hectic emergencies, seldom getting sufficient sleep, the better Jacobins, unlike Bonapartists and Stalinists, were optimists, irresistible in euphoria, though liable to break unexpectedly. They were bronzed with phrases which dazed not only posterity but themselves. 'The words we have uttered will never be lost on earth.' (Saint-Just). Danton, the first military saviour, Trotsky of 1792, was a verbal volcano. 'The Kings of Europe threaten us. We cast at their feet the head of a King.' Rhetoric easily becomes not the slave but master of thought, though its opposite too has liabilities. 'It is the opinion of my committee that a further investigation should be undertaken, taking into consideration all those matters of which, in the opinion of the new committee, consideration should be taken.' (Neville Chamberlain)

Jacobin enthusiasms were mostly generous. 'One must keep the social contract by Virtue, not by force.' (Saint-Just) Robespierre's 'The French People decree the Liberty of the World' matches Lenin's 'We shall now proceed to establish the Socialist order.' No determinists, they believed in perfectability: not faulty humanity but faulty government originated crime. 'When all men are free they will be equal, and, when equal, just.' (Saint-Just) They yearned for the simple society. 'Happy is the country where punishment is a free pardon.' That it would probably be a very unhappy country does not detract from Saint-Just's exuberant good-will.

Their erstwhile allies, the Girondins, had grander financial interests, were adept in social graces and academic debate: the Jacobins, mostly unknown lawyers and unpublished intellectuals, attracted—like Hitler—the smaller tradesmen, discontented professional men, the noisy, though unreliable mob. They can *now* seem ridiculous in their melodrama—'Tear out my heart and eat it: then you will be what otherwise you will never be. Great.' (Saint-Just) 'Show my head to the people. It's worth it.' (Danton)— in their Roman poses in which David painted them, devising 'Classical' ceremonies—processions, lictors and fasces, white oxen with gilded horns, goddesses rising from pyres, allegorical statues, youngsters in chitons dancing round trees of Liberty, magistrates in togas. Jacobin art anticipated the Bolshevik. 'Painting must elevate man, inspire him and lead him on to noble deeds.' (Khrushchev)

Nevertheless, from June 1793 to July 1794 the Jacobins governed France as never before, solidifying the dreams of Philip the Fair and Louis XIV. Nominally responsible to the Convention they ruled through two Committees, Public Safety and General Security, and the police: forerunning Lenin's Polit-Bureau and Mussolini's Grand Fascist Council. First Girondin, then Jacobin, the First Republic anticipated the Napoleonic State: centralized, efficient, anti-feudal, Roman. In over 11,000 decrees, which indicated rather than fulfilled, the Jacobins abolished colonial slavery (restored by Napoleon I), began reforming Law, public health, primary education, polytechnics, communications, weights and measures: redistributing land, emancipating Jews, nationalizing the Church, fixing wages, confiscating for the poor, democratizing the army, establishing hospitals, orphanages, museums, art galleries, conservatoires, conscriptions, the decimal system. After an abortive 'Religion of Reason', the Supreme Being, a particular favourite of Robespierre, was restored, Maximilien himself, unwisely, leading yet another 'Roman' festival.

Like Bolsheviks, Maoists, Francoists, they eliminated all other parties, independent unions, corporations, and refused to free national minorities. Saint-Just asserted that Party Politics were only the choice between one crime and another. Similarly, General Franco was to affirm that 'Political Parties only divide the people.' (1971) Like the Bolsheviks, they destroyed their own Moderates (Dantonists) and Anarchists (Hébertists) in rigged Show Trials which had already condemned the King and Girondins. Like Stalin they issued a democratic Constitution, never operated.

Cruelty increased, less from planned wantonness than from the erratic dynamics of power. Though a few were sadists, most Jacobins and Bolsheviks were neither gangsters nor moral hooligans, though involuntarily fermenting ample conditions for both. Dominating not through superior morals but superior efficiency and force, they were swiftly outraged to find that virtue, civic sense, self-sacrifice, even rich harvests, do not arise automatically from virtuous legislation. They demanded absolute moral change and relative social revolution, neither as easy as pamphlets had suggested. Shootings, drownings, deportings, beheadings were wholesale, often irresponsible. Civilian 'Representatives on Mission'—Saint-Just was one—anticipating the Bolshevik Commissar, controlled the armies by terror.

Jacobinism ordained the Marxist and Nazi view of Law not as an impartial survey of evidence but as an adjunct of political struggle. Justice was the prerogative not of truth but of power. Slaughtering the SA, 1934, Hermann Goering proclaimed, 'Fellow Germans, my methods will not be crippled by any bureaucracy. Here, I do not have to worry about justice. My mission is only to destroy and eliminate, nothing more.' It may

Josephine Crickmay *Supervision 1794* 1971. The hot Jacobin summer of 1794 bred fantasies of blood and terror that frequently became literal.

have suggested a swaggering freedom and panache. For Stalin, 'the State is an instrument in the hands of the ruling class for suppressing the resistance of its class-enemies.' The Larger Good becomes not an argument but a cult. 'Collisions and discrepancies between the formal commands of the Law and those of the proletarian revolution must be solved only by the subordination of the formal commands of Law to those of Party Policy.' In grey prose rubbing out lives themselves grown grey, Stalin's Public Prosecutor, Vyshinsky, presiding at the Show Trial of the Old Bolsheviks, Lenin's comrades, was repeating Jacobin policy.

The Laws of Prairial and Suspects gave

the Committees right to execute on denunciation alone, before a packed Court, putting lives at the mercy of local vigilance committees, spies, blackmailers, the malicious. If a creditor suspected one's revolutionary ardour, it could be fatal. Moral guilt, a consensus of opinion of the paid, revolutionary juryman, outweighed proven guilt. 'He who trembles is guilty.' (Robespierre) Lenin was to affirm, 'The success of the Revolution is the Supreme Law.' It is part of Hitler's contempt for actual human beings. 'Their understanding is feeble. All effective propaganda . . . must not investigate truth objectively.' (*Mein Kampf*)

By 1794, the Jacobin Public Prosecutor, Fouquier-Tinville, boasted that heads were falling like slates off the roof. Political violence throws up such figures as Fouquier, Beria, Eichmann, hitherto without achievement, often devoted fathers, cosy husbands, sentimentalists, but secretly desperate for self-assurance, recognition, a name, preferring to be criminal than nothing. With clerkish, nerveless obedience, they assiduously hunt down fellow humans, exhilarated or intrigued not by life but by the mounting pattern of death. They became machines. 'A hundred dead is a catastrophe. Five million dead is a statistic.' (Eichmann, 1944)

Tudor and Stuart England had used show trials and Acts of Attainder to destroy political leaders. The French Terror was novel in the aggregate and variety of its victims: 30,000, some six per cent of them aristocratic, to be seen in the perspective of the succeeding White Terror, Napoleonic battles, the 20,000 Communards killed in one week, 1871: the perhaps 40,000 killings of collaborators by the Resistance, 1944–5, which included torture and eye-gouging: the nine million drowned or diseased victims of the Atlantic slave-trade. J. M. Thompson suggested that the Terror was negligible beside the French shootings, imprisonments, censorship, during World War I.

Nevertheless, extreme powers generally

Eichmann on trial 1961

record progressive moral degeneration. Fouché, Jacobin terrorist, later Napoleon's Police Chief, who began with 'absolute belief in the omnipotence of Human Reason, in Unlimited Progress,' superintended the shooting of several hundred young people in Lyon. Few withstand temptations to suppress others' opinions. 'Burning is not replying, Robespierre,' Desmoulins cried bitterly to his old class-mate, soon to be his executioner, who, as a calf-lawyer had once resigned office rather than demand the death penalty and was now declaring that 'the Revolutionary Government owes its opponents nothing but Death'. Saint-Just, former humanitarian, in stark nakedness of language, announced, 'In a Republic, which can only be based upon Virtue, any pity shown towards crime is proof of treason'—paralleled by Lenin's 'We must wipe off the face of the earth all traces of the ideas of the Mensheviks and Social Democrats who speak about individual rights'; and by the Chinese propagandist (August 1966), 'Kindness to the enemy is cruelty to the Revolution.'

The Jacobin Committees, by no means filled only with Terrorists, showed no inclination to relinquish power. On the contrary, they next deprived Deputies of the Convention of immunity from arrest. A triumvirate, Robespierre, Saint-Just, Couthon, 'The Madman, the Boy and the Cripple', was increasingly identified with the Terror: Robespierre, a nervous Puritan, visibly lapsing into an intolerance which interprets minor query as blasphemy, reasoned opposition as a threat.

They seemed alternately impatient and despairing, unable to understand or accept what their contemporary, De Sade, realized so well: that, instead of the good and the logical, man may deliberately choose the bad and irrational. De Sade was the real revolutionary, for whom, as for Freud, God and Devil, Revolution and Counter-Revolution, were big names to disguise sullen, unconscious Nature at war with herself, her vital contradictions creating society. Curiously, the Jacobins, for all their classical bric-à-brac, overlooked the Greek who voted for the expulsion of the great magistrate Aristides, from weariness of hearing him called 'the Just'.

Robespierre convinced himself that he was the infallible revolutionary guru; those who rejected his teaching were thus wrong, to be eliminated, like sickness. A sinister glamour lit the neat mediocre figure and weak voice that had shattered huge Danton. Robert Southey considered him a ministering angel sent to slay thousands in order to save millions. Some demented women hailed him as Messiah, 'the Son of Man'. In Buchner's play, *Danton's Death*, he is accused of always sacrificing others, never being sacrificed himself. During his ascendancy the French executed their finest poet, Chénier, and best scientist, Lavoisier. 'The Revolution,' Robespierre reassured, casually, 'has no need of science'. It was Stalinism in miniature. Under the Bolsheviks famous writers withered: Blok died of starvation, Mayakovsky, Yashvili, Tsvetaeva killed themselves; Mandelshtam, Babel, Pilnisak, Tabidze, Tarasov-Radionov, Kolstov were shot or died in prison: Pasternak and Solzhenitsyn silenced. And 'Vavilov, the most distinguished geneticist that Russia has produced in modern times, was sent to perish miserably in the Arctic because he would not subscribe to Stalin's ignorant belief in the inheritance of acquired characteristics.' (Bertrand Russell, *Portraits from Memory*)

Though Bolsheviks and Jacobins both demanded dictatorship, the latter mostly favoured private property, merely wanting it distributed more equally and used less selfishly: they confirmed the peasants' seizure of land which the Bolsheviks, implacably hostile to private ownership, finally, and bloodily, rejected. The Jacobins, while obsessed with the Rights of Man, were, like Napoleon I, Mussolini, Hitler and, indeed, like traditional religions, unconcerned with those of women: the Bolsheviks early granted women complete legal equality 'to free them from domestic serfdom'.

Both used Terror. The summer of 1794

saw a further Rule of the Elect. Though Terror largely ceased in the provinces, hundreds a week were still being executed in Paris, which, like the Convention, seemed numbed.

Hardly ever did one of these unfortunates try to struggle against his fate, even at the last moment. This curious paralysis testified to their consciousness not only of the immense power of the State but also of the elemental force of the Revolution, to which men succumbed as if to a force of nature. 'The condition of paralysis,' said a contemporary, 'was so strong that if one had said to a condemned person, 'Go home now and wait for the cart which will come round to-morrow and fetch you,' he would have gone home and next morning at the appointed time would have climbed onto the cart. (Friedrich Sieburg, *Robespierre*)

It recalls the Western democracies' paralysis before Hitler, 1933–9. Dostoievsky held that the most fundamental Russian quest was a craving for suffering, that deep in Russian consciousness is a feeling that you deserve to be flogged. A Chekhov character says that the Russian loves recalling life but does not love life. For Nietzsche the Germans 'will always obey, and will do more than obey, provided they get intoxicated in the process.' The French, though periodically prone to intoxication, have, since 1789, like a professional divorcee, briskly shed régimes that have exhausted their purpose. France produces not only humourless incorruptibles, but also those like Fouché, Barère, and Barras who wish to survive and are thus closer to popular feelings. This was neglected by Saint-Just and Robespierre. Both loved 'Mankind', 'the People', but the one despised his fellow-men and the other objected to them.

Their syllogisms were crisp but increasingly ferocious. 'The Terror is nothing more than Justice, prompt, severe and inflexible. Therefore it is an examination of Virtue.' (Robespierre) Government is skill: the idealists were making it butchery. The summer dragged on, quivering with heat and blood. Yet time turns sarcastic, bronzed phrases turn to slogans, history melts to myth, politics to theology, boring everyone. The professional experts on the committees were growing restive. Terror had been justified, and they had not begun it, yet their colleagues seemed now to be continuing it not because of visible emergency but from personal vendettas. Like cruel schoolmasters, the triumvirate, failing in argument, reached for the cane, and reached too often.

Handsome Saint-Just, 'Archangel of the Revolution', was known to be preparing a new and drastically austere political programme, probably a new proscription. 'The indifferent are as guilty as traitors and must be punished.' A dismaying gloss on *Revelation*: 'I know thy works, that thou art neither hot nor cold, but because thou art lukewarm, and neither hot nor cold, I will vomit thee out of my mouth.' Political zealots disdain to ponder *Ecclesiastes*: 'Be not righteous over-much, neither make thyself over-wise. Why shouldest thou destroy thyself?' Saint-Just's sincerity, that 'Some people have an appalling conception of Happiness and confuse it with Pleasure', would not long appeal to those who insisted on remaining French.

The Ends-Means morality, so acceptable against emigrés, profiteers, deserters, spies, black marketeers, against King, Girondins, atheists, was moral humbug against the Old Jacobin heroes, Danton and Desmoulins. And it threatened to go further. Political summits are liable to induce paranoia. The ruler fears his own colleagues, must reassure himself with purges. Having crushed opposition he must constantly find scapegoats for failure or threat of failure. 'To be safe we must kill everyone,' Hébert had said. Fouché would invent conspiracies to satisfy Napoleon's fears. Stalin died during the bogus Doctors' Plot, having just shot twenty-four Jewish writers for 'conspiracy', on behalf of international Jewry.

Robespierre was now speaking of a new conspiracy. Remembering everything, he forgave nothing. The enemies without had been famously repulsed, but there always

seemed more and more within. He became dizzy, trying to count them. Fouché, a face at the table, or vanishing round a corner, Danton's ghost. He sulked, kept aloof while, out of earshot, whispers began that there were no enemies, only dislike of Virtue and of the most virtuous of all.

The uncertainty endangered Fouché, whom even Napoleon was to handle carefully. It alarmed businessmen who wanted a stable exchange and markets. The mob wanted lower prices and was tiring of spectacle. Boredom is fatal to systems. In Committee Carnot, 'Organizer of Victory', taunted Robespierre and Saint-Just as 'ridiculous dictators'. Conceivably they were only ridiculous. The pair again denounced 'the conspirators' but foolishly refused to name them. When at last they were about to do so, the Convention nerved itself to shout them down. Saint-Just accepted it in proud indifference, Robespierre vainly attempted to shout back. 'The blood of Danton chokes you', a voice cried. Within forty-eight hours they were dead, trapped in peculiar irresolution, through despair, moral fatigue, or, suddenly, over-scrupulous about legality. The great talkers died in silence which still provokes speculation and drama. Madame Roland had perished, literally talking her head off, the words noble, the effect negligible as cottonwool falling.

Jacobinism dissolved in blood and White Terror. 'Yes, Robespierre, there is a God', a bystander said, over the corpse—unfairly, after Maximilien's efforts for the Supreme Being.

Like contemporary Russian leaders, and perhaps Mao, Robespierre, while operating within a dictatorship, was not himself a dictator though many thought he was, as he too may have done. Like Mussolini, he was easily overthrown, by intrigue and an instant of courage. An amateur of power, he remains ambiguous, perhaps tragic: an acidity of personality mingled with something singular but indefinable, separating him from others, blurring his reputation. He lacked the flexibility of Caesar, Lenin, Mao, the coarse realism of Napoleon I and

Robespierre contemporary portrait. No revolutionary figure was further from the popular legend of howling terrorism drenched with blood and ardour.

Mussolini, the pleasant manners of Napoleon III, the ability of all these to use a common touch they may not always have felt. He was more akin to Stalin, at ease neither with people nor the People. His idealism is unquestioned, but was no substitute for bread. He seems never to have laughed. He would not have smiled at Burkhardt's remark that in 1793 people wanted not to be communists or socialists but new owners of stolen goods.

Conceivably Napoleon had a fleeting memory of Robespierre on the eve of his Russian invasion. 'I feel myself driven on towards an end that I do not know. As soon as I shall have reached it, as soon as I shall have become unnecessary, an atom will suffice to shatter me. Until then, not all the powers of humanity can do a thing against me.'

France bitterly debated Robespierre's bicentenary, 1958. A Revolutionary deputy, Baudot, had written, 'Robespierre's power was very strange. It rested on a public opinion he had deceived, on the spell of Terror, and on fanaticism.'

For the Goncourts 'the eighteenth century fashioned men for Society, the Revolution fashioned them for the State.' Talleyrand, fastidious, intelligent, supple, exemplifies the first, using events to enrich himself yet substantially benefiting his fellows. Had Robespierre been more corruptible he might have lived longer. Alternatively, regarding men as fools, demons or ciphers, he was the most corrupt of all.

To Talleyrand the Jacobins must have been ludicrous, madmen, self-righteous and ill-mannered. They left behind a permanent revolutionary myth, of blood, proscription, rhetoric, a red lustre of progress blazing up in 1830, 1848, 1870. In the Algerian crisis, 1958, a 'Committee of Public Safety' was formed in Algiers. Students rioting against Gaullism, 1968, established a 'Club des Jacobins' and 'Committee of Public Safety', even demanding a meeting of the Estates General.

The secret dream of a good many Frenchmen, and the majority of French intellectuals, is a guillotine without the victim.
André Malraux *Anti-Memoirs*

Hitler read Trotsky with admiration: Himmler studied Tsarist and Bolshevik secret police. The Bolsheviks regularly discussed the Jacobins, determined to avoid their mistakes. They too wanted a complete break with the evil past, and found it too difficult. They too dedicated themselves to 'the People' from an idealism largely middle-class. They too overthrew (November 1917) a government eloquent but vacillating in administrative chaos and military danger. They too accomplished immense material achievements and made political and moral mistakes of such enormity that they can seldom be discussed without fervour or analysed with certainty. Their Revolution gave hopes to millions of the disinherited. Does it still?

That the 1917 emergency justified temporary dictatorship is probably proven. In the brief Constituent Assembly the Bolsheviks were in a minority of one to four.

Placed as they were, the Russian communists developed into a permanent ruling class or oligarchy, recruited not by birth but by adoption. Since they could not risk the growth of opposition they could not risk genuine criticism, and since they silenced criticism they often made avoidable mistakes; then, because they could not admit that the mistakes were their own, they had to find scapegoats, sometimes on an enormous scale.

George Orwell

Lenin—the name cuts like a whip—remains more controversial than Caesar or Napoleon I. Some maintain that Paul and the Church corrupted the gentle purity of Jesus: that Stalin and the Party betrayed Lenin. This is doubtful. The Gospels show Jesus as passionate and intolerant as most inspired youths: Lenin accepted Marx's belief in force as the midwife of progress. Like Jesus he uttered marvellous apologia. 'These children', he told Gorky, 'will have much happier lives than we had . . . there will not be so much cruelty in their lives . . . and yet, I don't envy them. Our generation achieved something of amazing significance for history. The cruelty, which the conditions of our life necessitated, will be understood and vindicated. Everything will be understood, everything.'

Lenin stands for a technique, as evidence for the individual's role in history. With profound and terrible clarity he knew what he wanted. He applied nineteenth-century Marxism—international, theoretical, designed for industrialized States—to agricultural Russia whose growing industrialism had been shattered by war. Robespierre had

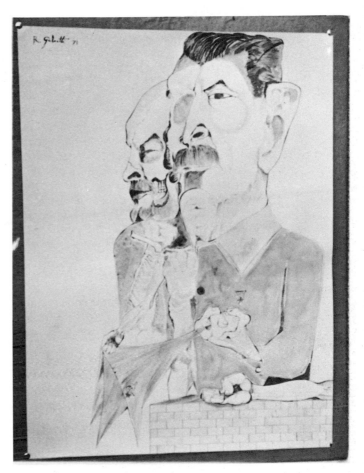

Renzo Galeotti *Twin Growth* 1971. Lenin and Stalin, seen not as opposites but as brothers-in-rule, conditioned by a common ideology.

accepted Rousseau not as a suggestive poem but as a literal political handbook: Lenin consistently sacrificed theory to practice. He sawed deep. Christopher Hill (*Lenin and the Russian Revolution*) notes that when somebody mentioned 'peasants', he alone saw not a vague mass but three distinct classes and interests. His tactics towards them, confirming their land-seizure, withdrawing it, then restoring it, were decisive. Schoolmaster as well as activist, he never ceased repeating that Revolution depended on live soviets of workers and peasants rather

69

than bureaucrats, and that Liberal Parliamentarianism was incapable of generating the energy. He grasped to the full Marx's dictate 'the philosophers have only interpreted the world in various ways. The point, however, is to change it.'

Long before 1917 he set himself to transfer 'the Revolution' from an academic hope to the practical goal of a small élite. Against Mensheviks and many Bolsheviks he insisted that trained cadres were more useful than mass votes, and that dirty work must not be shirked. 'A scoundrel is of use to us precisely because he is a scoundrel.' (Churchill on occasions said the same.)

Master of tactical detail, Lenin's rigorous intellectualism enabled him to master the long view. His apparent inconsistencies held true to the inner consistency, the safeguarding of the Revolution, which, under him, and the brilliant though amateurish Trotsky, remained fluid and, almost to his death, hopeful.

Hill shows him defending a proposal to discontinue his cherished municipal soviets, arguing that this would test their efficiency: a good soviet would never allow itself to be dissolved. Like Trotsky, he was an internationalist, loving the great bourgeois novels, envisaging the fuller freedoms. 'Communism should not bring asceticism but enjoyment of life and vigour in life through a fulfilled love-life.' This is unlike Stalin, and Hitler, mistrustful of normal, popular pleasures, even condemning co-education.

Lenin held that absolute revolution was absolutely essential, to be expected only from those wholly uncompromised with Tsardom. Liberal intellectuals, rich peasants (Kulaks) would never wholly reject a régime that had benefited them. Willingness to compromise had made European Social Democrats prefer patriotism to international socialism, voting the war-credits in 1914.

Lenin was abroad when the Tsar abdicated, but his return changed, against all expectations, a moderate constitutional Menshevik Republic to a Bolshevik dictatorship which accomplished total military victory against the Whites, began nationwide electrification, rehousing, social insurance, domestication of wild youngsters; established crèches, libraries, schools to banish mass illiteracy. (When the slaughter of the Imperial Family at 'The House of Special Purpose' was announced to the Supreme Praesidium, Lenin said, after a short pause, 'Let us continue reading, clause by clause, the draft of the Public Education Bill we were discussing.') Women entered all masculine strongholds save the top political—medicine, law, teaching, engineering, journalism, at odds with Mussolini's view that war is the most important male activity, as maternity is a woman's: at odds with the Nazi relegation of women to cows, to Church, nursery, kitchen and bed: at odds with D. H. Lawrence, 'Ottoline has moved men's imaginations and that is perhaps the most a woman can do.'

Lenin's death at fifty-three probably helped his reputation. His 'Wonderful Georgian', Stalin, has been blamed for all the subsequent disappointments. 'Only by fighting a battle of extermination against Social Democracy can one fight Fascism.' Stalin's words, but impeccably Leninist. Party zealots have loaded on Stalin, as Judas, a guilt that owes much to Messiah, Lenin. Stalin murdered Spanish Anarchists, Lenin had already disposed of the Russian. During the famine, 1932–3, with six million dying, Stalin exported Ukrainian grain to buy foreign machinery. Lenin had done likewise. Stalin's executions still contaminate socialism: Lenin permanently dissolved the Constituent Assembly, liquidated all other parties, opponents, anarchists. 'The Mensheviks say, "We have always said what you are saying now: permit us to repeat it again." We say in reply, "Permit us to stand you against the wall."' Lenin trusted only the Elect, perhaps vainly gambling on his own survival, to transcend them in a better future.

Revolutions are made by fanatical activists, men with one-track minds, men narrow-minded to the point of genius. They overturn the old order in a few hours or days. The whole upheaval takes a few weeks or at most years, but for decades thereafter, for centuries, the spirit of narrowness which led to the upheaval is worshipped as holy.

Pasternak, *Dr Zhivago*

Revolutionary violence builds on that of its predecessor. Lenin shot the former heroes, the Kronstadt sailors. 'If Life is sacred, we must abandon the Revolution,' said Trotsky, who, in 1917, unsuccessfully tried to break his promise to the Czech Legion and arrest it after it had by agreement surrendered arms. The Tsarist Anti-Terrorist Okhrana, with spies, informers, provocateurs, secret police, was retained and developed by Lenin and still exists, as the deadening, unscrupulous, million-strong KGB. Secret police are independent of régimes, attracting not idealists but a certain perennial psychological type. As a temporary expedient the censorship was restored. Tolstoy wrote of *The Raid* (1852) that 'it was simply ruined by the Censor. All that was good in it has been struck out or mutilated.' His translator, Aylmer Maude, added, 'Not content with striking out three passages, the Censor demanded the insertion of sentences he considered desirable.' The contemporary Russian novelist Anatole Kuznetsov, who fled to England, stated (*Sunday Telegraph*, 3 August 1968): 'My first book was published twenty-five years ago. In those twenty-five years not a single one of my works has been printed in the Soviet Union as I wrote it. For political reasons the Soviet censorship and the editors shorten, distort and violate my works to the point of making them completely unrecognisable. Or they do not permit them to be published at all.'

Lenin continued capital punishment: Soviet Russia has more capital crimes than Tsarist. The great humanist in effect negated revolution by strengthening the intolerant Party and bureaucratic clamp on education, communications, law and national minorities. 'It was the supreme expression of the mediocrity of the apparatus that Stalin himself rose to his position.' (Trotsky, *My Life*)

No one, Saint-Just had admitted, can reign innocently. Athenian democracy destroyed Socrates, made cruel imperialist wars. Whether Lenin could have genuinely resisted the destructive tendencies within his ideology, whether he could have cut loose from centuries of Russian and European repression, whether, deep down, he wanted to, remains unanswerable. His last months, secluded and crippled, showed misgivings. He had selected and promoted Stalin, now Party Secretary, into a position more powerful than Trotsky and Bukharin recognized. In a posthumous memorandum, suppressed, to his widow's anger, beginning, 'I am strongly guilty before workers of

George Grosz *At the Barrier* 1921–2

Alison Morgan *Power* 1971

Russia . . .' Lenin advocated the replacement of Stalin by someone 'more tolerant, more loyal, more civil and more considerate'.

Whether fulfilling or poisoning Lenin's intentions, Russia was moving far from the testament of the murdered German communist, Rosa Luxemburg. That ideals, unaccompanied by executive responsibility, are easy to utter does not mean that they should not be uttered.

Determined revolutionary action coupled with a deep feeling for humanity, that alone is the real essence of Socialism. A world must be overturned, but every tear that flows and might have been staunched is an accusation; and a man hurrying to do a great deed who knocks a child down out of unfeeling carelessness commits a crime.

These words could have been written by the novice John of Leyden, Robespierre, by Lenin himself. One might agree with H. G. Wells who did not deplore the Russian Revolution because it was a revolution: he complained that it was not a good enough revolution and wanted a better one.

Marx had demanded the dictatorship not of a man but of a Party on behalf of 'the proletariat'. Victorian, authoritarian, pre-Freudian, he disregarded any party's aptitude for jealousies, feuds, irrationality, surrendering to war-god or High Priest.

Red Russia has more universities than Tsarist: Tsarist student life was arguably freer. Tsarist law-courts had, in major political cases, to prove guilt by convincing a jury. Both régimes share endemic anti-semitism and fits of Terror.

Red Terror in Russia, Bavaria, Hungary, facilitated, as in 1848 and 1871, White Dictators—Horthy, Pilsudski, Mussolini, to 'save society'. 'Electoral Reform' in Russia destroyed Parliamentary discussion; 'Land Reform' reduced the peasants to state-serfs; 'Liberation' has engulfed the anti-communist Baltic States and sent tanks, secret police and executioners into Budapest and Prague. As under the Jacobins and Napoleon I, 'the Revolution' changed from international brotherhood to national imperialism dressed as 'world-revolution'. Leninism, even before World War II, seemed no convincing answer to that other Left, Anarchism, so hated by Marxism as a rival for the socialist soul, and for whom Proudhon spoke, maintaining that no government can ever be called revolutionary, for the very simple reason that it is the government.

An active internationalist social democrat, of the type so condemned by Marx, Lenin, Stalin, yet of more impressive moral stature, and who could consistently supply workable alternatives to the 'either-or' fantasies of all three, wrote:

It has always seemed to me curious and confusing that communists are accepted on their own classification, as Extreme Left. Their political outlook and organisation is more like that of the Catholic clerical parties on the continent, the old Centre Party in Germany, and the present Christian Democrats in Italy, and of the deceased Fascists and Nazis: i.e., their correct classification is slightly to the right of the extreme Right.

Leonard Woolf, *Downhill all the Way*

The Dictator Controlled by Power

What is the world, soldiers?
    It is I:
I, this incessant snow,
    This northern sky;
Soldiers, this solitude
Through which we go
    Is I.

Walter de la Mare

Du nom qui oncques ne just au roy gaulois
Jamais ne fut un foudre craintif,
Tremblant l'Italie, l'Espagne et les
    Anglois,
Du femme estrange grandement attentive.*

Nostradamus (1503–66)

He solves the scientific problems posed by the preceding process of intellectual social development: he points the way to the new social needs created by the preceding development of social relationships: he takes the initiative in satisfying their needs. He is a hero. But not . . . in the sense that he can stop or change the natural course of things, but in the sense that his activities are the conscious and free expression of this inevitable course. Herein lies all his significance: herein lies his whole power. But this significance is colossal and the power is terrible.

Plekhanov

i

A Dictator may, like Tito, know when to stop, or, like Napoleon III, slightly withdraw: like the Jacobins, like Khrushchev, he may be arrested in full cry, as a public nuisance: like Mussolini or Primo de Rivera, he may be sacked by a hitherto nominal Head of State. Others are tempted to a further role, 'Roman Emperors', 'Gods on Earth', 'World Conquerors', drugged, like Redeemer Nkrumah, by excess of dream, overwhelmed by forces they should be controlling.

Though the Dictator is not, his temptations are superhuman: to succour like a god, yet maintain human relationships: to enrich society without enriching himself: to give orders without being thrilled by them: to accept the tensions of ageing: to restrain impatience: to keep on the earth, free from crazed 'Inner space'.

For he is superstitious grown of late,
Quite from the main opinion he held once
Of fantasy, of dreams, of ceremonies.

Julius Caesar

John of Leyden proclaimed himself 'King of the World'. The Menshevik Kerensky, deposed by Lenin, thus a suspect witness, was still convinced (1970) that Lenin's 'Idea' was to become supreme world leader through a world revolution, at the cost of generations of Russian dead.

Napoleon I had Jacobin sympathies that did not survive his experience of the People in action. 'We have finished with the romance of the Revolution, we must now begin its history.' Cynical and realistic, he added that the Revolution was concerned not with Liberty but with Vanity. His own career, however, was concerned more with the history of Napoleon.

Napoleon was not original as soldier or politician; he was original in himself, with abnormal memory, concentration, control over sleep, self-discipline, decision. Unlike Hitler, and Napoleon III, but like Caesar, he enjoyed hard work. Impatient with

---

*Of a name known to no French king before him, never was a thunderbolt so frightening, making Italy, Spain and England tremble. He will pay great attentions to a foreign woman.

Jacques-Louis David *Napoleon Crossing the Alps*
1800. A painting that dominated the huge Romantic
Exhibition in the Tate Gallery, London, 1959.

obsolete customs, an impatience which perhaps made him habitually cheat at cards, he erased the picturesque, obscurantist, destructive. He was practical. In Egypt he insisted not only on glory—'Twenty centuries look down on us', he cried, at the Battle of the Pyramids—but hygiene. He continued the Convention's modernizing and coding a Law essential to middle-class, anti-feudal advance—like Roman Law, the Code Napoleon is lucid, precise, though more authoritarian than British Common Law—centralizing education, liberating

From *Napoleon* 1925. The hungry, austere futuristic young Napoleon, still far from the stout Emperor with eyes and face increasingly dulled.

Jews, building hospitals, ordaining juries (though these were to be nominated, not chosen by lot), eliminating clericalism, improving communications, replacing aristocracy with meritocracy, then abolishing the Spanish Inquisition (twice restored after his departure).

Following his third plebiscite, he assumed the Imperial Crown, with court, Grand Huntsman, Grand Almoner, Arch-Chancellor, Grand Chamberlain, a new nobility, the Legion of Honour. None knew better than he the value of advertisement, particularly among illiterates. At Erfurt he ordered loyal demonstrations: at these, proclamations were brandished. 'If God's Son dwelt amongst us, He would be called Napoleon.' He exploited and bullied the Pope: like the Nazis he looted the European art galleries. His murder of the Duc D'Enghien was a gesture to shatter royalism, not punishment of the guilty. Propaganda was unremitting. 'In war, considerations of morale make up three-quarters of the game: the relative balance of man-power makes up only the remaining quarter.'

The Old Monarchy had been a work of art, involving emotion and politics, religion and secularism, personality and bureaucracy. To Napoleon, like everything else, it should be re-polished, not abolished. For a Beethoven, the Napoleonic Crown was an outrage on Revolution, Rights of Man, the liberating promise of the hungry young General Bonaparte himself, an eighteenth-century solution to nineteenth-century problems. But Napoleon probably considered that human nature was constant, still hypnotized by the ancient magic symbols of power. He seldom miscalculated, though when, during the Hundred Days, he appeared not in the familiar grey coat and hat but in resplendent imperial adornments, people were disappointed or repelled. Doubtless the Empire also gratified his own operatic qualities. Certainly it symbolized a process in his withdrawal from reality, leaving him as 'Roman Emperor' perched too high.

His limitations were as formidable as his talents. He lacked capacity for friendship and cooperation, alienating Talleyrand who could have been the Empire's choicest asset: 'a lump of dung in silk stockings', Napoleon called him. He did not discuss, he stated, or harangued. Not only did he refuse to tolerate equals, he refused to acknowledge that he had equals. He disliked sensible advice, was a professional liar. 'It is difficult to decide what is the most remarkable thing about Napoleon—his generalship or his lack of humour.' (Lytton Strachey) A good Italian, he could not escape his own family, so that, against his better judgement, he planted them on thrones, on which most of them refused to grow. An aggressor, he was impatient with civilian manners—tact, patience, finesse. He would not have delighted Plotinus: 'He is no great man who thinks it is a great thing that sticks and stones should fall, and that men, who must die, shall die.' To the Duke of Weimar he confided that he felt at ease only in war. Balzac remarked that he inoculated himself with armies. At Elba, after haggard disasters in Russia, he declared, 'Je suis né un être tout à fait politique; je n'aime ni la femme ni le jeu.' This is not a corollary of dictators: John of Leyden, Kemal, Mussolini, Danton, Napoleon III, Riza found 'worldly' an admirable word, and puritanism and austerity are seldom qualities of a satisfactory ruler. (Of Edward IV, Sir Thomas More wrote, 'He was of youth greatly given to fleshly wantonness', adding, 'this fault not greatly grieved the people.')

Compared with Talleyrand, Goethe, Burke, Stendhal, Schiller, Fox, Sheridan, Byron, Chateaubriand, Wellington, Louis XVIII, his mind was uninteresting. On a complaint that the Empire lacked poets he said he would consult the Minister of the Interior. He could talk with the sham profundity of a Hollywood epic: 'When one looks up at a starry night, can one doubt the existence of God?' His callousness is dispiriting. To Metternich (1813): 'I may lose my throne but I shall bury the whole world in its ruins.' In 1814, 'A man such as I does not worry his head about the lives of a million men.' He is comparable to Hitler, 1945, raging that without victory the Germans had no right to survive. 'He was as great as a man can be without morality.' (De Tocqueville)

Napoleon thought sufficiently of himself to impose his will on millions of Europeans, but, like Stalin, his view of their possibilities was warped, without faith in peaceful democratic change. Dictatorship usually presupposes a static world. Napoleon himself, once an image of purposeful movement, master of technology, became indifferent to economic and technical novelty. He saw no future in steam-power. Creating a chance for European unity, he sacrificed it for French domination, like Hitler treating associates like victims, so that in crisis he could rely on little foreign or progressive support. His greatness was in the greatness of the opportunities he missed.

Bonapartes often decayed early. By 1809 Napoleon seems to have lost some physical and mental vitality, compensating through fantasy and megalomania. Thenceforward he became not a serious ruler but hero of necromancy, romance, myth. He did men a disservice by presenting misleading conceptions of greatness. He revitalized education in terms of the traditional paternalist family, not to foster curiosity, self-fulfilment, sheer fun, but obedience, national unity, utilitarianism. Equality under the Law degenerated into equality under Napoleon, though the Law survived him. His secondary schools were headquarters of a nationalist cult, so that Michelet could later affirm, 'One People, One Fatherland, One France'. He illustrates the poverty of a dictatorship that overstrains itself and the crowd, seeming to extend human potential but encouraging delusions, sycophancy, and substantially reducing the male population.

His drama precipitated a mass of imaginary selves, in fiction, paintings, lonely bedrooms, of vast dreaming men above the Law, indulging unseemly behaviour, new Alexanders rocketing through prosaic facts, soaring to the heights in J. L. David's breathless picture, Bellerophon irresistible. He appeared another enthralling proof that

Fate was a matter of superhuman will-power, of choice. 'What have we to do with Destiny?' he asked Goethe, without waiting for a reply; 'Policy is Destiny.' And indeed even his political destiny did not end at St Helena but re-emerged (1849) in grim proof of the human credulity and the lure of the colossal that he knew so well. His wars, like an over-heated conservatory, stimulated aggressive nationalism in France, Germany, Italy. For many, he discredited the eighteenth-century belief in Progress, yet for generations more was written of him than of any other historical figure save Jesus. For Byron, the three greatest men of the century were Beau Brummell, Napoleon, and himself.

Lytton Strachey (see Michael Holroyd, *Lytton Strachey*) reversed this. 'The embodiment of all that is vilest in the character of mankind—selfishness, vulgarity, meanness, and falseness, pushed to the furthest possible point—that so many people should have admired him so much seems to me one of the bitterest satires on humanity. It is the ape admiring its own image in the looking-glass.' Dr Johnson's verdict on Charles XII of Sweden, that he was extraordinary without being great, seems apposite. 'What a pity,' Talleyrand murmured, 'that so great a man should have been so badly brought up!'

That 'Napoleonic' is no longer always praise may mean no more than that with new education, or lack of it, people have forgotten the original Napoleon while still clustering round imitations.

ii

Napoleon I effected useful changes, Napoleon III helped the workers, Stalin and Mao built factories, Hitler roads. The question remains—not always requiring the same answer—whether the methods are the only ones available, were they worth the

Goya *They Are of Another Breed* from 'The Disasters of War'

Goya *Why?* from 'The Disasters of War'

Goya *On Account of a Knife* from 'The Disasters of War'

cost, what were the motives, whom did they benefit? None of them would have had patience with Queen Elizabeth I, herself authoritarian but flexible, realistic, pragmatic, marvellously and maddeningly human: 'I seek not windows into men's souls.'

Benito Mussolini reverenced Napoleon I, kept a bust of him, fashioned himself in Napoleonic mould. Something of a United Italy had been briefly restored by Napoleon, revived by Napoleon III, completed 1870. It had not, by 1918, overcome corruption, poverty, weak government, national disappointment. In 1896 had been humiliating military defeat by Ethiopia. Bribed into the Allied Cause, 1915, largely by secret agreements subsequently disowned, Italy lost more than men. 1919–22 saw nationalist and Red terrorism, strikes, mockery of war veterans and, in Italy, feeble parliaments under an undistinguished monarchy.

Mussolini, blacksmith's son, vain, yet self-mistrustful and gauche, superstitious, capable of humour and occasional self-insights, former socialist, eleven times jailed for political rampages, was not, despite ferocious phrases and a war-wound, an impressive soldier, even falsifying a passport to avoid military service. His part in 'The March on Rome' (1922) was by train, after its conclusion. A journalist of flamboyant talent, he had literary ambitions, writing a noisy play, and a novel, *The Cardinal's Mistress*.

Marx and Engels had not been immune from stock German nationalism. In 1849 Engels was recommending 'a pitiless fight to the death against Slavs, traitors to Revolution, a war of extermination, terror without scruple, not in the interests of Germany but in the cause of Revolution . . . the coming World War will wipe from the face of the earth not only reactionary classes and dynasties but reactionary peoples as well. That also forms part of progress.' (See Richard Hare, *Pioneers of Russian Social Thought*) His war would have extinguished the chances of Lenin and Stalin. Neither he nor Marx, however, foresaw the nationalist

dictators supported by the petty-bourgeois together with nervous property owners and declassed or deprived monarchists, forces antipathetic to internationalism, collectivism, proletarian virtues. Marx's 'Workers have no country' proved nonsense in 1914, and still does. Interviewed on Haiphong Island (*The Observer*, January 1967) about the meaning of Marxism, a leader of the North Vietnam Workers' Party replied, 'In the first place it is complete devotion to one's country.'

Fear of the Left stimulated the Right. Napoleon III, 1851, had struck his *coup d'état* to save the State from 'Red terror', by then no longer very real: the Reichstag was burned down, 1932, in a crisis of Nazi fortunes, suggesting a plot to capitalize on fears of communism. Hitler, June 1933, was vaunting himself Saviour of Europe from Bolshevism. Mussolini, 1922, was spreading rumours of a Red plot, when Italian communism was actually declining.

He had founded a Fascist, Black Shirt cohort in Milan, 'To Believe, Obey, Fight', as a patriotic, disciplined protest against parliamentary incompetence and international malice that had frustrated Italy's 'legitimate' territorial demands as a war victor. Exploiting a parliamentary crisis, with its renewed fears of strikes and civil war, he sent 30,000 Fascists to Rome to save the situation, and, with royal connivance, remained in uninterrupted power until 1943, the year when Juan Peron, admirer of Hitler and Mussolini, successfully led a March on Buenos Aires.

The Duce was never a systematic thinker, perhaps was proud of it. A rumbustious orator he was better at orchestrating the music of power than at producing blueprints for a better society. 'Fascism is a movement of reality, truth, life adhering to life. It is pragmatic. It has no *a priorisms*. No remote ends. It does not promise the usual idealistic heavens. It does not presume to live forever or for long.' (1919)

His one-party State achieved understanding with the Vatican that sanctified his invasions of Abyssinia (1935) and France

(1940). It was not, like the Nazis, pagan, but emphasized the crusading, heresy-hunting aspect of Catholicism, together with battle-cries about 'God's Purpose' and 'Destiny'. The Fascist Grand Council usurped most of the parliamentary rights, with the Duce responsible only to the King. Trade-union independence was abolished, forcibly joined to management as a branch of the 'Corporate State'. Law, press, radio, and education were similarly coerced. Like Horthy, Franco, Hitler, Peron, Mussolini retained but exploited Private Property: major industrial policy was controlled, the State interfered at will, lock-outs and strikes were forbidden. Both for propaganda and to relieve un-employment, spectacular public works were initiated: roads, irrigation, reafforestation, Roman archeological excavations, electric plants. Ezra Pound, connoisseur of bright surfaces, presented (*The Cantos*) Mussolini as avatar of Odysseus, the Cid, Sigismundo de Malatesta, symbols of virility, social renewal, cultural metamorphoses.

'Maqvesto'
Said the Boss, 'è divertente',
Catching the point before the aesthetes
    had got there;
Having drained off the muck by Vada
From the marshes, by Circeo, where no
    one else wd have drained it.
Waited 2000 years, ate grain from the
    marshes:
Water supply for ten million . . .

From *Yellow Caesar* 1941. Hitler and Mussolini.

Poverty had wrung Italy for centuries. Mussolini wished her to be self-supporting by expanding agriculture and industry, particularly cars. Like Hitler, he used re-armament as unemployment relief. The New Roman Empire in Abyssinia was not only to avenge 1896 but to provide work and homes for new white colonists.

Like Napoleon III, Mussolini began his régime with intimidation: the bludgeon, the castor-oil dose; exile, prison, and assassina-tions—of his most resolute opponent, Matteotti, the newspaper editor, Amendola —and, again as with the Second Empire, his country under him enjoyed, for a decade, economic and moral recovery and international recognition, at the cost of civil liberties and legal opposition.

'The nation was glad of his coup d'état . . . when in December, 1922, twenty-two Italian communists were murdered in their homes, the murderers were congratulated by the Under-Secretary of State and amnestied by the judges.' (J. Hampden Jackson, *Europe since the War*)

Like Hitler, Mussolini postured as if in autobiographical opera: the tunes were to become more recognizable than the meaning, which had begun with brutal clarity. 'Man is free only in and through the Whole: the

David Low *The Difficulty Will Arise When Someone Wants To Go Somewhere* 1937

Whole can only be a sovereign State which tolerates no discussion, no control.'

A sense of Fascist movement and efficiency long misled important foreigners. Lord Butler admired the early Corporate State. Thomas Edison rated Mussolini 'the greatest genius of the modern age'. The Liberal H. A. L. Fisher's *History of Europe* (1936) contains the following sentence: 'The re-markable character of the Italian leader, the way in which he succeeded in correcting the fatigue and despondency of the Italians and in harnessing to the use of the State all the military virtues which had been educated by the War, his skill in striking the popular imagination, in generating enthusiasm and confidence, and his success in overcoming industrial unrest, attracted sympathies in other countries and led to the formation of Fascist groups or parties.' For the Press-Lord, Rothermere, he was 'the greatest figure of our age'. (1928) Winston Churchill saw him as a crusader against 'the bestial appetites of Leninism'. 'I have been charmed as so many people have been by Mussolini's gentle and simple bearing and by his calm

82

detached poise.' (1926) By 1937 he was praising Mussolini's 'amazing qualities of courage, comprehension, self-control and perseverance', almost none of which Benito actually had.

Britain and France, traditional friends of Italy, mishandled Mussolini, and, against all Italian history and probably to his own misgivings, helped tilt him towards Hitler.

The New Rome was a failure. Autarchy wrecked the economy: Ethiopia was costly and unprofitable; corruption and brutality created disillusion. Intellectual response was negligible. Modern dictatorship has had no place for a Cicero, Victor Hugo, Croce, Toscanini, Thomas Mann, Stravinsky, Casals, Einstein, Lorca, Pasternak. . . .

Mussolini, boastful and superficial, had increasingly believed his own ranting articles. 'The biggest bluff in Europe', Hemingway had called him, at the start. His private world sunk into fantasy, where he now appeared a dangerous child playing with toys too large for him. The corrosive make-believe in which Emperor Caligula had 'conquered Neptune' by employing his expensive army to throw stones at the sea. The swirl of unending marches, vainglorious salutes, archaic imagery. 'No painting is worth a banner captured from the enemy,' stated Foreign Minister Ciano, Mussolini's son-in-law whom later he shot, for treachery. He liked being photographed half-naked, but his bare torso remained a uniform, sometimes a breast-plate.

The Duce became mesmerized: by Hitler, whom he despised, resented, ultimately feared: by himself—children sat under his portrait, as if under a saint, garnished with 'Mussolini is always Right', an estimate of human ability which would provoke world-wide ribaldry.

A Napoleon III, a Mussolini, yearns to be taken seriously, as Law-giver, as Restorer of Glory. With the wind behind him the Duce exhorted the Italians to be less sympathetic, to become 'hard, implacable, hateful: masters'. Violence is often a solution for those with too little imagination to count the cost, or those with too much who do not

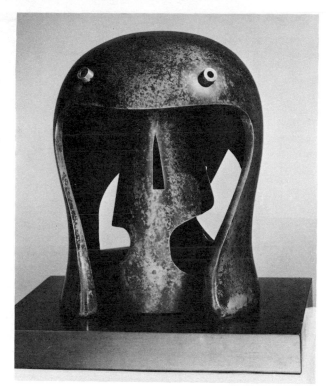

Henry Moore *Helmet Head no. 1*

realize that there is a cost. The brain ceases to be a muscle and becomes a self-indulgence. The Ethiopian campaign spattered Italy with odium: defenceless villages were gassed and burnt, black notables dropped alive from planes: the Duce's son boasted of 'good sport' shooting peasants from the air. The dignity of the black Emperor Haile Selassie shamed his noisily exultant conqueror.

Mussolini's career underlined the absurdities of power and moral heat. The French revolutionaries had lopped steeples, for equality, paraded an actress in Notre Dame as Goddess of Reason, forbidden hand-clapping as 'worthy only of slaves'. A Fascist circular demanded the abolition of hand-shaking. 'Apart from every consideration of a Fascist character, it is unrealistic, wastes time, and causes embarrassment owing to the inevitable conclusions that derive from it.' Sex is conscripted into political ethos. The Nazis established stud-farms to perfect blue-eyed Aryans. Burmese communists (1953) replaced 'You are beautiful, I love

David Low *Haunted* 1940

you', with 'I am profoundly impressed by your qualities as a loyal and vigorous Party Member and desire to wage the Party struggles beside you.' They forbid horse-racing but encourage golf. Chinese Red Guards (1966) denounced 'Eyes Right' as counter-revolutionary, and (1968) the First Secretary of the Kwantung Party Committee announced, 'In the grand Mao Tse-Tung era, guided by Mao's Thought and the infinitely superior Socialist System, chicken feathers can undoubtedly ascend to heaven and may already have done so.' From Russia (1971) *Nedelya* reported that a Chinese marriage is a chance to study Mao's works and maintain a permanent domestic atmosphere of ideological struggle and criticism.

'To live in a country without a sense of humour is unbearable; but it is still more unbearable to live in a country where you need a sense of humour.' (Brecht) Democracy, of course, not always harmless, has its own comedies. Presidential campaigns, royal occasions, priests blessing bombers, parliamentary verbiage. 'Ah, my friends,' Ramsay Macdonald sighed, 'how easy it would be to listen to the milk of human kindness!'

'Mussolini is not only my friend but my master, my chief. He has awakened dreams in my spirit and in the spirit of millions of Germans.' (Hitler, 1938) Führer and Duce, 'Hit and Muss'. Hitler prudish, theory-ridden, Mussolini a Danton without the stuffing, did not in fact have much in common, though the former, rather pathetically, was loath to recognize the Duce's rapid wartime decline.

Both dictators felt themselves closer to the People through mass rallies and acclamations than by routine constitutional processes. 'I swear to execute the orders of the Duce without discussion' was obligatory to all Italians at the age of fourteen: similar oaths were exacted from the Hitler Youth and the Young Communist League. The pair shared with Stalin the apparatus of infallibility, censorship, secret police, hatred of unofficial art and literature. All three believed in the Rights not of man but of selected categories of men. All could rely on a cowardly, passive, though secretly jealous army. Generals, said Marshal MacMahon, are always those who have the least courage to act.

Despite Roman bombast, Mussolini

hesitated to enter the World War until convinced that Hitler had won it. His attitude towards the soldiers is unendearing. 'I needed some thousands of Italian dead to enable me to sit at the peace-table as a belligerent.' While Goering wrote to Ciano:

We cannot worry unduly about the hunger of the Greeks. It is a misfortune which will strike many other peoples besides them. In the camps for Russian prisoners they have begun to eat each other. This year between 20 and 30 millions will die of hunger in Russia. Perhaps it is as well that this should be so, for certain nations must be decimated. But even if it were not, nothing can be done about it. Obviously, if humanity is doomed to die of hunger, the last to die will be our two peoples.

Nothing more discredits a Dictator than his view of people as digits, relevant only to the Idea which, theoretically, exists to benefit them. Malraux (*Anti-Memoirs*) reports Mao's words to Nehru about an atomic 'Socialist' war.

If half humanity was destroyed the other half would still remain. But, in return, imperialism would be wholly destroyed and only socialism would still remain on earth, and within ten years or a hundred

From *Yellow Caesar* 1941. Mussolini.

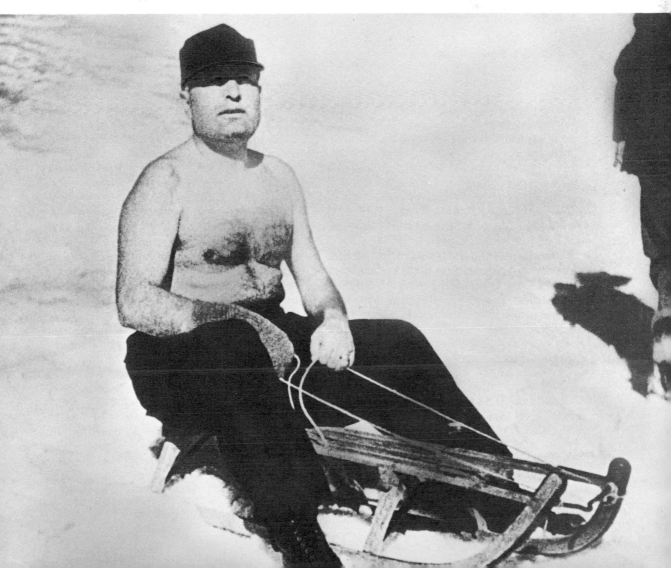

Bronze helmet probably 1st century BC. Taken from the Thames at Waterloo Bridge.

the population would again grow, by even more than 80%.

It is the attitude of the Assyrians, who made fine roads, but for armies: had irrigation, coinage, libraries, but to fetter, not quicken, the mind.

In Greece, North Africa, Italy itself, the Germans had continually to rescue the Fascist armies. A British officer in North Africa reported captured 'Five acres of Italian officers, forty-seven acres of men'. Mussolini relapsed into alternate apathy and grandiloquent wishful thinking: advertisement, not leadership. Meetings with Hitler were intolerable humiliations. The Grand Council finally revolted: the King, torpid since 1922, sent the Duce to a hill-top prison from which he was daringly rescued by the Germans and reinstated as dictator of a North Italian puppet republic. In final defeat, 1945, he fled with his mistress—like Napoleon III he had been an arduous womanizer—was hunted down by partisans, shot, not without dignity, his carcase left hanging upside down in the Piazzale Loreto, Milan, like raw carrion.

He had written his own epitaph (1944) in a mood that suggests that one could perhaps have done business with Mussolini:

> One day History will weigh up the balance and say that I built many buildings, many streets, that I threw many bridges across rivers; but it will have to confess that as far as the spirit is concerned we were only common pawns in the general crisis of the human conscience, and that we remained pawns until the end.

Fascism has revived in Italy, with some electoral success. For the Duce, a curious postscript. In 1971 his widow was still managing an eating-house near Rimini, selling, with irony unconsciously apt, Beefsteak Benito, Spaghetti Blackshirt, Spongecake Fascist Empire.

iii

'Fascism is the exaltation of the executioner by the executioner: Russian communism is the exaltation of the executioner by the victim.' (Camus, *The Rebel*)

The Bolsheviks had to galvanize a people for centuries apathetic, lazy, drunken, sometimes savage, sometimes affectionate and servile, sometimes as if moonstruck with marvellous discrepancies, but always venerating God and Tsar as interchangeable moral entities. Stalin, from 1924–39, knew this with stubborn, obsessive vehemence that condemned the more imaginative Trotskys and Bukharins as shallow academics. At whatever cost Russia, like China, must become industrialized, literate, efficient, secure. Russian history had been a moral tale of foreign invasions, military weakness. Therefore, dams, tractors, oil-refineries, blast furnaces, armaments made chatter about individual rights an unforgivable treason. 'For with Communism as an idea the essential thing is not what is being done but why.' (Milovan Djilas)

Stalin can be credited with impressive statistical feats: whether Stalinism was the only possible way is the question. The achievement, not only through the gigantic setback of the War, is equivocal. Mass industrialization and scientific education enabled such technical masterpieces as the first Sputnik, but did nothing to encourage humanist curiosity and political freedom. Collectivization has left Russia still having to import food from the despised and decadent West. More social services have not reduced the secret police. Education remains authoritarian, puritan, propagandist.

Stalin himself remains oblique and remote, Byzantine, not Roman. Judgement here is personal and provisional. He never publicly ranted, his writings were impersonal, his methods secretive. Like Napoleon III he was taciturn and shifty. Like Hitler he had a brutal and unsuccessful father (from a family recently serfs). Technician, not inspirer, he fulfilled Dostoievsky's yearning for the Tyrant Judge. Unlike Mirabeau, Danton, Saint-Just, Lenin, Trotsky, Mao, he seems never to have dreamed nobly. For him, revolution was less liberation than revenge. Without much zest for life, he told Malraux that in art he liked only Shakespeare and 'the Dance'. Actually, he read widely. He enjoyed drinking and, like the Duce, Laurel and Hardy. (Hitler disliked Mickey Mouse, mice were 'dirty'.) He would never have agreed that the right to assent can be more productive than the obligation to obey.

Before 1917, Stalin had been revolutionary agent, writer of Georgian nationalist verse, bank robber, terrorist. He had known betrayal and exile; there is talk too, unsubstantiated, of his having been a Tsarist informer. During Civil War and invasion he, like Mao and Saint-Just, showed personal courage and party devotion; later, he showed adroitness in reconciling, then coercing, secessionist minorities. In the war crisis, 1941, he, almost alone of the Russian leaders, remained in Moscow. His temperament kept him silently filing, annotating, watching, while Trotsky (a late Bolshevik), Bukharin, Tomsky, Zinoviev made exciting speeches.

He was never a charmer. A poor Georgian without intellectual fluency, he must have felt morose before Lenin and his brilliant middle-class lieutenants. For him, as for Robespierre, 'the Revolution' may have had

to replace the unsatisfactory father and awkward human relationships. Like Napoleon I he distrusted workers, colleagues, experts alike, increasingly believing only in his own despotism. For foreign revolutionaries he was as contemptuous as Mao is of amateurs like Guevara. Like Hitler his foreign policy was conditioned by ignorance and uninterest in foreigners. He backed Chiang Kai-Shek against Mao, despite Chiang's medieval cruelties to captured Reds: he instructed German communists to regard the Social Democratic Republic as more dangerous than the Nazis, with whom tactical collaboration could be permitted. His expressed justification (1931) was Russian security irrespective of socialist cant. Thus the invasion of Poland (1939), war with Finland, the pact with Hitler himself.

The Pact can be defended as a desperate follow-up not only of his own prejudices but of insulting rebuffs from Britain, France, Poland. Whatever his demands, which probably included the Baltic States, they could scarcely have exceeded the horrors of the War.

Expediency, cynicism, ignorance, narrowness, cowardice infected all countries, 1926–39; Stalin may well have dourly felt that a fellow-dictator, Hitler, spoke his own language more readily than a Daladier or Chamberlain. Lord Halifax, the patrician British Foreign Minister—to whom a visit to Hitler was acceptable, to Stalin, not—had expertise no less culpable. 'If we had to choose between Poland and Russia, Poland would give the better value.' Stalin's crime was less in the Pact itself than in believing, against all historical and psychological evidence, that Hitler would respect it.

To see the entire West, bourgeois and Nazi, destroy itself, while preserving his own masterful inactivity, appeared both righteous and shrewd to the guardian of 'the Revolution'. Moscow denounced Britain and France as aggressors in an imperialist war, advised workers to sabotage factories and generally weaken 'plutocratic democracy'. Russia dutifully supplied essential materials to the Nazis, handed German communist refugees

Churchill and Stalin at Yalta Conference 1945

back to the Gestapo. 'The Soviet Union is interested in preventing the Allies from realising their war-aims—the destruction of Hitlerism.' (Molotov, 1940)

Whatever Stalin's stature as a war-leader he had responsibility for almost four years of German savagery in Russia: ravaged provinces, destroyed cities, a siege of Leningrad costing nine thousand killed and starved a day, mass exterminations. He ignored all warnings of German invasions, notably from the old anti-Bolshevik, Winston Churchill, to whom 'as far as strategy, policy, foresight, competence are arbiters, Stalin and his commissars showed themselves at this moment the most completely outwitted

bunglers of the Second World War.' (*The Grand Alliance*)

German armies and SS invaded, 1941. Churchill, with some complacency, continues: 'Thus the ravings of hatred against Britain and the United States which the Soviet propaganda machine cast upon the midnight air were overwhelmed at dawn by the German cannonade. The wicked are not always clever, nor the dictators always right.'

Stalin was not warlike, or rather, he used aggression most largely against his own people. For a régime proud of its freedom from superstition, exploitation, immorality, its bloodshed is unbecoming. Policies were a matter of police. None of Lenin's first Polit-Bureau died naturally. Of Soviet police chiefs until 1953, two were murdered, two vanished, five were executed, the last, Stalin's henchman, Beria, being shot, after his master's death, for treasonable killings and for being 'a British agent'. Khrushchev claims that of the 139 members of the 1934 Central Committee, ninety-eight were shot: of the 1966 delegates to the 1934 Party Congress, 1100 were shot. 1937–8, the entire Ukrainian Polit-Bureau was shot. The much-praised Moscow Metro and Moscow-Volga Canal were built by slave-labour.

The Communist camps were not for brute killings but to provide labour for mining, lumbering, farming, building. There were no criminal medical experiments and sterilizations, bayonetings, gassing of children, though (7 April 1971) Moscow Radio accused Maoist China of killing twenty-five millions in ten years and consigning millions more 'to immense concentration camps'. Russian deaths were often due to overwork and primitive conditions rather than to policy. Thousands of Kulaks perished building the White Sea Canal. On Stalin's death, fifteen to eighteen millions were in slave-labour camps at Karaganda, Vorkuta, Norilsk, attacked by Khrushchev at the 20th Party Congress. GULAG, central organization of the concentration camps, still exists.

Stalin, like Robespierre and Himmler, was impaired by theory, which allowed no deviation. No more than Hitler did he anticipate universal freedom. He sneered at 'Those who imagine that Socialism demands Equality, equality in the needs and private life of citizens. These are petty-bourgeois views of our Left-wing nit-wits.' Lives and values were mere responses to changing politics: truth—in law, linguistics, genetics, agriculture, history—was strategy. Objectivity was heresy. Like Robespierre, Stalin seemed to identify the political situation with his own situation. A supreme Dictator, he would not admit the social value of variety: in ideas, work, art, morals.

In agonized economic crisis, Lenin had reluctantly allowed private farming, originally the supreme inducement to attach the peasants to the revolution. To Stalin, as to Castro, that a man might dig his own field more zestfully than the community's was either untrue or unworthy, anyway economic nonsense. Thus the richer peasants, Kulaks, must be dispossessed. Kulaks—the word,

'Fist', is uninviting—were popularly considered usurious and grasping: much of Tsarist Great Russia, moreover, had a tradition of communal farming. But the subsequent anti-Kulak campaign led to vaster casualties than the Crimean and Franco-Prussian wars, perhaps five millions being 'liquidated', far exceeding even the notorious deaths on the Somme. Perhaps a crude parallel can be made with the long-drawn-out English enclosures, the cruelty, injustices, evictions and joblessness being subsequently justified by claims of more efficient land management and production.

Stalin's second wife is said to have killed herself in horror at the cruelties, as Castro's sister left Cuba in protest against the executions. We do not know the depths of Stalin's Socialism. For Djilas, once an admirer, even devotee of Stalin, pretence was, with Stalin, so spontaneous that it seemed that the dictator himself became convinced of the truth and sincerity of what he was saying. 'He has the glory of being the greatest criminal in history.'

David Low *Rendezvous* 1939

Stalin, seconded by Khrushchev, was a purger: of Party, People, Army. Six to seven millions were shot or deported east, 1936–8: three to four million, 1944–5: without public trial.

The Soviet Union is justly reckoned the model of a multi-national State . . . all the more monstrous are the acts initiated by Stalin which crudely violated the basic Leninist principles of the nationality policy of the Soviet State. We refer to the mass-deportations from their native places of whole nations.

Thus Khrushchev, at the 20th Party Congress, 1956, at which he denounced the dead dictator for military disasters, illegal cruelties, disregard of human rights. Yet at the 18th Congress, Khrushchev, who had ably assisted Stalin in just this, notably amongst Poles and Ukrainians, had continually referred to 'Our Great and Glorious

Stalin . . . Glory to our Great Stalin . . . Leader of Genius'. Under such a system words languish: sycophancy promotes no excellence. Only bearers of endless good news pass the censors in the palace and in the dictator's own mind. 'In times of revolution,' Danton had said, 'I see that power falls into the hands of scoundrels.' Stalin's successors could safely admit the 'improper methods' used to force Jewish doctors to confess murder of the Party official, Zhadenov. André Gide wrote (1936), after visiting Russia, 'I doubt that in any country to-day, even in Hitler's Germany, the spirit is less free, more cowed, more terrorised, more of a slave.'

One of the purged, the poet Osip Mandelshtam, wondered, 'Why is Stalin so afraid of genius? It is like a superstition with him. He thinks we might put a spell on him, like shamans.' His widow, Nadezhda, in *Hope against Hope*, remembers, 'We all took the easy way out by keeping silent in the hope that not we but our neighbours might be killed.' Another poet, Yessenin, dying

Victory Day, Berlin 1945. General Patton and General Zhukov take the salute.

by his own hand, wrote a final poem in his own blood.

The threat of the century is government by dossier, filing-cabinet, data-bank, controlled by a mediocrity, Beria or Himmler. In the grotesque confessions and condemnations of the Russian purges was no pure, thrilling, Dantonesque indignation. Prosecutor and victim alike were dulled by toneless and fouled authority, exchanging rehearsed dialogues in weary inescapable drill, all feelings save cunning, fear, confusion smothered by powerlessness to make taut authentic choice. A monotonous dehumanization, like the 7370 windows of the Pentagon, the 40,000 telephones, 32,000 officials, twelve daily tons of waste paper.

In *The First Circle*, Solzhenitsyn interprets Stalin as intolerant not only of inefficiency but of over-efficiency, which menaced his own absolute superiority.

The terrible thing about Stalin was that if you made a mistake with him, it was like mishandling a detonator—it was the last mistake of your life. Stalin was terrible because he never listened to excuses. He never even accused you; the only sign was a malignant gleam from his yellow-tigerish eyes and a slight puckering of his lower eyelids. Inwardly he had already passed sentence without the victim even being aware of it: he would be allowed to leave, he would be arrested the same night and by morning he would be shot.

Like head-waiters, dictators are convinced of their own indispensability. Khrushchev reports Stalin addressing the Polit-Bureau, 1950. 'You are blind, like young kittens. What will happen when I am gone? The nation will die, because you are incapable of recognising enemies.'

Bertrand Russell maintained that, after the emancipation of the serfs, 1861, Tsarist Russia had 'a thousand times more freedom than Stalin's'. Visiting Stalin's Russia he found 'a close, tyrannical bureaucracy with a spy-system more elaborate and terrible than the Tsar's, and an aristocracy insolent and unfeeling composed of Americanised Jews.' (*Autobiography*, Vol. 2)

Simultaneously Stalin attracted an admiration cult, not proved but asserted by Western intellectuals, who either, like Shaw and the Webbs, denied his terrorism, or excused it, perhaps sanctioning disagreeable traits in themselves. Because of his socialist objectives he had, apparently, freed himself from brutal power-politics: contrary evidence was erroneous: all would later be explained, no longer in a State but in a brotherhood created by Stalin. The Russian 'comrade' was infinitely superior to the English 'mate'. Like present-day Ché, Castro, Mao, Stalin was identified as avenger of the poor, punisher of the damned. Stalin, wrote Bernard Shaw (*New Statesman*, 1934) 'has delivered the goods to an extent that seemed impossible 10 years ago; and I take off my hat to him accordingly.'

This idolatry of Stalin's personality, as well as more or less everything in the Soviet Union, acquired irrational forms and proportions. Every action of the Soviet Government—for example, the attack on Finland—and every unpleasant feature in the Soviet Union—for example, the trials and the purges—was defended and justified. What appears even stranger, Communists succeeded in convincing themselves that such actions were right and proper and in banishing the unpleasant facts from their minds.

Milovan Djilas

As 'Uncle Joe' he benefited from a second, salvationary wartime Russian heroism. Afterwards, his ambiguity returned. His 'anti-imperialism' added by force twenty-four million non-Russians to the Russian State and bloodily controlled four major satellites. His theology made him refuse Marshall Aid for those who most needed it, simultaneously demanding from them vital capital goods for Russian reconstruction: a theology akin to the Jacobin Carrier's, 'We would rather render France a cemetery than not regenerate her in our own way.' He remained obdurate, suspicious, implacable, at Kremlin parties indulging in drunken horse-play not from conviviality but as private tactical manoeuvres. The United States and Britain refused their atomic secrets to the man accused of the Katyn mass-murders, who had coldly refused assistance to the Warsaw anti-German rising, dishonoured his Yalta pledge for free Polish elections, broken safe-conducts. In his huge survey of the Russian Revolution, E. H. Carr concludes that: 'The grandiloquence of Napoleon III, the cynical diplomacy of Cavour, and the blood-and-iron discipline of Bismarck were all reflected in the dictatorship of Stalin.'

Stalin must not be judged as a lapsed democrat, a liberal apostate. Historical appearances must be dissolved. He never escaped the onus of being a human being within a thousand-year tradition profoundly undemocratic. The new century had created no new dispensation. Proper Nouns—Church, Age of Faith, Youth, Christian Tradition, Socialism, CIA, Modern Man—deceive by being accepted literally, instead of as grand names for commonplace struggles, sometimes subterranean, always formidable, occasionally poetic.

'Money is stronger than despotism.' (Napoleon I) Timon reflects, 'This yellow slave will knit and break religions.' Thus medieval Catholic Hungary and Poland together fought the Catholic Teutonic Knights: Christian Portuguese were given absolution to fight Christian Leon. Bloody Mary's Catholic government refused to restore the monastic lands that enriched Catholic and Protestant alike. Notaras, a Greek Orthodox Byzantine statesman, would repeat 'Better the Sultan's turban than a Cardinal's hat.' Richelieu supported Protestant Sweden against Catholic Austria. 'If God exists,' Pope Urban VIII remarked, 'Cardinal Richelieu will have much to answer for. If not, he has done very well for himself.' It is easier to profess beliefs than to believe in them. Few Tudor Catholics would have welcomed a Spanish Catholic invasion: few English Catholics, 1940, were clamouring for Mussolini. Stalin's Russia, nationalist and imperialist, was arrogant and bullying to Red Yugoslavia.

'This yellow slave . . .' The Society for Propagation of the Gospel branded its West Indian slaves with SPG. The Portuguese slave-traded from Fort Jesus. At Jutland, the British used German telescopic sights delivered from Zeiss through Holland. Austen Chamberlain admitted, 1926, that British firms had in war-time sold arms to enemy Turkey. Allegations (1970) that the Vatican had shares in Institutio Farmacologico Sereno, which makes The Pill, were not contradicted.

When, on the eve of the German attack on Russia, the United States ambassador asked Winston Churchill, 'arch anti-communist', whether he could morally support the Soviet Union, Churchill replied that he had only one purpose, 'the destruction of Hitler, and my life is much simplified thereby. If Hitler invaded Hell I would make at least a favourable reference to the Devil in the House of Commons.'

Stendhal (*Rome, Naples and Florence*) reports on this perennial relativity of values.

In later life—usually at about fifty—the priests of the Duchy either take to drink, or else to religion—the latter normally consequent upon the death of one of their mistresses: and when that happens, they voluntarily assume the most fantastic penances, and find relief in an attempt to persecute their younger colleagues. The customary reward is a fine display of public contempt and hatred. In 1792, when the emigré priests began to flood from France into Italy, Italian priests throughout the country were profoundly shocked by the restraint and sobriety of their lives.

Today Red Russia trades with White South Africa, indifferent to the apartheid practised against Black workers: built the Aswan High Dam and recouped the Islamic Egyptian army after its defeat by socialist Israel, though Egyptian communism was banned by Nasser and its leaders imprisoned. Anthony Eden's disdain of 'legal quibbles' in the Suez crisis of 1956 is comparable to Germany's contempt for 'the scrap of paper' in 1914.

An argument for dictatorship is that it can

Sir Basil Zaharoff, the international financier and munitions manufacturer, from Robert Neumann's *Zaharoff, the Armaments King* (publ. 1938). Knight of the Legion of Honour, knighted also by George V, Zaharoff became a man of mystery and legend, accused of arming all sides simultaneously in war and peace, and of having a baleful influence over Lloyd-George, particularly in the Greek-Turkish war 1922.

The new 'Swerdlow' bridge in Charkow 1938. Symbol of Soviet advancement, typical in its very featurelessness of the artistic achievements of dictatorships.

shatter bureaucratic red tape. Actually, this seldom occurs, it more often concentrates on political rather than human needs. Overworked, the central machine gets clogged. When law courts, universities, unions, churches, sport, laboratories, banks, youth movements are state-controlled, the imbalance of forces assists terror of initiative. A Cromwell tries to regard himself as senior executive of a collective council: more commonly, the dictator regards himself as in daily conference with God, or becomes God. The density of society is respected more than individual quality, the part sacrificed to the whole. Dissent has to be conspiratorial: dictators are thickened by dogma. Stalin wished to believe in Lysenko's theory of acquired characteristics, as added justification of collectivism: at a genetics conference, Lysenko praised Stalin as 'the greatest of all contemporary scientists'. Both misled themselves. Paradoxically, but true to the nature of life, Shaw, a Stalinist, maintained that every despot must have one disloyal subject to keep him sane, a view that Stalin himself constantly, and bloodily, refused.

Anatoli Fedoseyev, a Russian expert on the magnetism of electronic physics, who renounced his country, explained (*Sunday Telegraph*, 18 July 1971):

Soviet Science has few original achievements to its credit. The reason is that the scientist in Russia is in a constant state of conflict with the Soviet political system. The scientist needs freedom; the system demands discipline. The scientist needs scope for initiative and the play of imagination; but the Soviet rulers insist that he should concentrate all his efforts on certain fixed, narrow objectives. This is why most Soviet scientists are dissatisfied. The men who rule the Soviet Union are interested only in keeping power in their own hands. Anything which helps them to preserve their power has their support. Anything which appears likely to threaten their power is automatically condemned, and freedom is what they fear most of all.

There remains the consistent Stalinist belief that in the elimination of free elections, secret ballot, free communications, is victory for 'the workers'. It is less amenable to outside pressures, such as forced the British and French out of Egypt, 1956, the same year as the Budapest rising, at which 150 boys were captured, kept in prison until their eighteenth birthdays, after which 142 were shot, all protests unavailing. Also in 1956, General Giap, of the North Vietnamese Communists, stated, 'We have made too many deviations and executed too many honest people. We attacked on too large a front and, seeing enemies everywhere, resorted to Terror, which became far too widespread ... Worse still, torture came to be regarded as a normal practice during Party re-organization.'

In Cuba, March 1971, Herberto Padilla, a revolutionary poet, was imprisoned and subjected to humiliating 'self-criticism' of the Stalin-Mao design, confessing to conspiring, with named friends, for the CIA. This, May 1971, provoked an open letter to Fidel Castro from Sartre, Alain Resnais, Pasolini, Moravia, 'in shame and anger', accusing his government of extracting forced confessions, then pleading for the avoidance of 'the obscurantist dogmatism, cultural xenophobia, and general repression which Stalinism imposed on the socialist world'. Alternatively, discussions of Castro's Cuba may produce arguments for dictatorship as vehement and sincere as any of the century, ending in denials that the dictatorship exists. That it was produced by cruelty and inefficiency is surely undeniable. As for conditions within Russia itself, Solzhenitsyn has, in an open letter, attacked the practice of imprisoning sane dissidents in madhouses as *'spiritual murder*, a variation on gas chambers'.

It's true: there have been changes on the
    animal farm:
They used to strangle people in sacks:
Now the killing's done by modern methods
—With electricity. After all, it's cleaner.
                Yevtushenko

The Dictator in Control of Power

Nothing can be rushed. Things must grow, they must grow upwards, and if the time should ever come for the great work—then so much the better.

Paul Klee

The spiritual man ought from the start to oppose and repudiate revolution, for he knows how slowly any change of lasting significance is effected, how little apparent it is, to the point of invisibility.

Rilke

The risks of dictatorship are obvious. Pretending to expand human possibility by dynamic action, they more often contract it by coercion and standardization. They simplify life to formulae, speaking of 'masses', 'proletariat', 'nation', 'bourgeoisie', as if these were homogeneous in their needs and ideals. Lying is offered as a higher form of truth strengthened by noisy ukases. Dictatorship opposes too much that graces existence: wit, irony, eccentricity, experiment in art and behaviour. Like religion it holds that essential truth has already been established. It is cavalier about fair play, impatient with the crippled, intolerant of the weak or unusual, disgusted by the old. Burke's 'If I cannot have reform with equity I will not have reform at all' remains the classic riposte. Bertrand Russell would not sacrifice civilization even for social justice. Even under a benevolent dictatorship, movement is cautious, spontaneity disliked, values related less to popular welfare than to the stability of the régime, the régime which is rendered unnecessary in proportion to social advance. So the remedy is distorted to prolong the sickness. Beginning by hoisting people out of the mud, dictators end by finding much in favour of mud. Their

Mustapha Kemel 1935

instruments facilitate savagery. Tito, no Roman Emperor, actually decentralizing, unusual in a dictator, nevertheless allowed genocide against the Albanian minority: Ranhovic, his police boss, used torture and killing, notably in Djakovica. Tito has thrice imprisoned his old, outspoken colleague Djilas, who found himself 'in the dilemma in which every communist who has adopted the communist idea with goodwill and altruism finds himself. Sooner or later he must confront the incongruity between that idea and the actual behaviour of Party leaders.'

Renzo Galeotti *Bertrand Russell* 1970

Salazar ruled Portugal forty years in an atmosphere of quiet stagnation ('History is not made by anecdotes'), though the jails were fuller than they seemed. Such rule is seldom as efficient as logic suggests. Permanent concentration of power in an individual, even a philosopher-king, liable to old age and neurosis, is hazardous: in his enormous isolation failure entails enormous expenditure. Most dictators over-employ 'Divide and rule'; Stalin did, and notoriously Hitler, which contributed to the fact that Germany mobilized less industrial war effort than the democracies: Luftwaffe leadership was slovenly, outdated, at odds with itself: Army and SS hated each other: Party officials were corrupt: Bormann secured his rival Himmler a coveted and disastrous military command to reduce his standing with the Dictator. Personal antagonisms and racial irrelevancies obstructed atomic research.

Democracy cannot afford complacency. Since the Athenian massacre at Melos, it has known slave-trade, lynch-law, union-smashing, union-selfishness, industrial despotism, colonial tortures, exploitation, evictions, well-poisoning and evil camps.
We have got
The Maxim Gun, and they have not.
Goethe preferred support for a lie to political disorder. Democracies, oligarchies, aristocracies, have Huey Longs, Capones, Zaharoffs, Richelieus: government deceptions, foraging irresponsible power-combines and monopolies, militarists, those who tar and feather. Bigotry, intolerance, aggression are not confined to the retarded, paranoiac, psychopathic. The admirable Trollope wrote, 'Of the Australian black man we may certainly say that he has to go. That he should perish without unnecessary suffering should be the aim of all those who are concerned in the matter.' For General Sherman, 'The more Indians we can kill this year, the less we will have to kill next year.' Freud demanded the excommunication of colleagues who rejected his theory of the primacy of sexuality. During a famine Tolstoy pronounced that loving was more important than giving food.
Not all dictators have been scoundrels, nor their régimes worthless. Steven Runciman has suggested that, if absolute power corrupts, so does absolute powerlessness. In the human tumult dictatorship can sometimes, in crisis, be justified if it at once sets about building conditions for its abdication. Had Louis Napoleon contented himself with the presidency for ten years he might have retired with impressive achievement, even renown. This is demanding much: the reluctant dictator is uncommon, though a case could be made for Cromwell, and Madero of Mexico. Dictators, like the crowned monocrats, are capable of keeping their fullest strength in reserve, for tactics as much as magnanimity, but, for most, the Show must go on because they dare not let

it stop. Too many enemies abound, the dead demand retribution through huge eyes, power degenerates from responsibility to a narcotic.

Cromwell controlled messianic hooligans and Leveller extremists as firmly as he did royalists. Only in Ireland did he lose sanity. 'The moment the very name of Ireland is mentioned,' Sydney Smith said, 'the English seem to bid adieu to common feeling, common prudence, and common sense, and to act with the barbarity of tyrants and the fatuity of idiots.' Cromwell wanted more universities, not necessarily for indoctrination. Yet, a running sore of autocracy, he evaded the real problem of the successorship, trusting, against all evidence, that the English would prefer his son, 'Tumbledown Dick', to Charles II.

Many latter-day dictators similarly rose from army commands. Marshal Pilsudski (1863–1938), the first President of the Polish Republic, severely nationalistic, competent administrator, was, like Cromwell, fretful of constitutional feuds and political deadweight, though, for both, power implied more a job of work than a heroic pose or fantasy.

An unknown Persian colonel, Riza Pahlavi (1877–1944), angrily resented Anglo-Russian threats to his backward, weakly-ruled, oil-wealthy country. A nationalist military coup, 1921, soon left him dictator under the young Shah, becoming Shah himself, 1925, elected by a Constituent Assembly. Thenceforward, the army remained more effective than elections. Riza reformed its medical departments, enforced conscription, added an air-force. Like Kemal a Westernphile, Riza determined to modernize a slow ancient country long dominated by over-privileged feudalists, bandits, quarrelsome tribes, dishonest officials, impoverished and grievance-ridden workers and peasants, obstructive Islamic institutions. His despotism abolished female seclusion and the Veil, restrictive Moslem courts: built railways, roads, airports, schools, hospitals, a university, national bank; reduced foreign influences and brigandage.

Such a temperament does not voluntarily relinquish power. He enjoyed wealth, giving orders, lugging people into the present. Contempt for others' ability and mistrust of intellectualism suggested another, though more impressive Mussolini. With censorship, subservience, packed parliaments, he ruled fiercely and unquestioned until World War II. Though perhaps favouring Germany more than the old oil-imperialists, Britain and Russia, faced with German infiltration and general threat to the oil-fields, he desired neutrality. This was unrealistic: Britain and Russia jointly invaded, replacing him with his son, the present ruler.

Riza left Persia more prosperous than when he found it. Stendhal's judgement on Louis XIV, that he stole away the judgement of his subjects and put it in his pocket, is often pertinent, but Persian judgement in 1925 was not profound.

Mustapha Kemal, 'Atatürk' (1881–1938), was son of an Albanian Serb, a customs official turned merchant. As a young, rough-mannered, nationalist radical officer, early jailed for sedition, even on active service he accepted the Young Turk Movement, the protest against the corrupt, effete Sultanate which had forfeited respect at home and abroad. Turkey's entry into World War I, on behalf of Germany, won Kemal national hero-worship as victor over the Allies at the Dardanelles, 1915. More than ever impatient, he grabbed further popularity and official hatred by denouncing the vindictive Treaty of Sèvres by which the now successful Allies tried to dismember the last slice of the Ottoman Empire. He dominated 'the National Organization', an armed party demanding nationwide reform, during the post-war defeat, with the Allies and the old Greek enemy occupying Constantinople, with martial law superimposed on parliamentary breakdown and court supinity. Outlawed, he was rescued by the Greek aggression, 1922; with the Sultan's government paralysed or in flight, Kemal and his nationalists triumphantly counter-attacked. By 1924 the Treaty was torn up, foreign troops gone, frontiers established, foreign

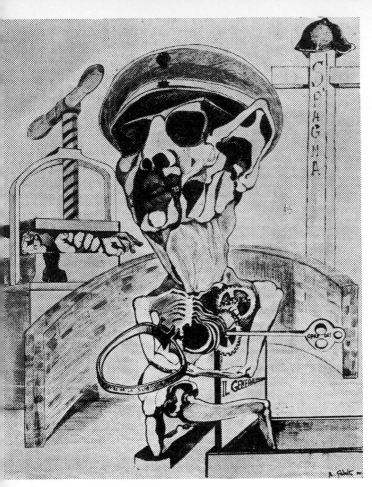

Renzo Galeotti *El Generalissimo* 1970

policies settled, Sultan and Caliphate abolished, with Kemal as President, Chief of the Council of Ministers, Commander-in-Chief, Leader of the People's Party.

His rule fulfilled three generations of Turkish radicalism, for which vanished imperial splendours were not 'Roman' gifts, but traps, to be recalled only in order to replace and forget them. Young Turkey denounced the past, Ottoman and Islamic, the powerful foreign communities, the lack of patriotic purpose. With passion, but not with passion alone, but decree, executions, beatings, Kemal ripped down spiritual and secular obscurantism. To break Islam, he abolished the Fez, Veil, Titles, as Peter the Great had outlawed the Orthodox beard and Shih Hwang Ti burned the classics. Like Riza, he secularized law and education. Like Lenin he secured women's emancipa-

tion from the home into the professions, women's suffrage bringing them into the National Assembly (1935) though, by its headlong suddenness, creating more dislocations than the men had anticipated. To such a man, all traditions were demonstrably bad: that some might supply organic psychic and practical links was irrelevant.

Complex Arabic script was replaced by the Latin, Kemal himself, sardonically, grimly, paternally, holding much-publicized writing classes. Technology, industry, railways, roads, state factories, state monopolies of key-goods, official support for exports and industries, anti-malarial and reafforestation schemes, a Civil Code on the Swiss model—smashed the aura of corrupt Pashas, absentee landlords, harems of useless, overweight women, official inertia periodically galvanized by cruelty. Cruelty remained, without the inertia.

Kemal, the Ghazi (Conqueror), was no communist. Uninterested in utopias, he used power for efficient workings of all State gadgets. He did not appeal to the destructive or irrational in people, he seldom appealed to the people at all, but methodically announced the next programme, the means for its fulfilment, the punishment for saboteurs. As against the bloodshot Soviet collectivization he replaced huge, badly-managed estates by small peasant-owned farms assisted by land-banks. He, no more than Stalin, had any Tolstoyan belief in peasant virtues, but, like the French, knew that a landed peasantry meant a stable conservative balance against restless towns. No successful revolution is initiated by peasants. He may have felt that individual land-ownership supplies a psychological and material incentive unusual in state-farms.

He too wanted freedom from devious foreign aid, though trading both with Russia and the West. He aimed to reconcile old enemies and lost provinces. Less happily, he required a one-race State, at the expense of long-established Greek and Albanian minorities. His expulsion of a million and a half Greeks is comparable to Louis XIV's ejections of the Huguenots and the early

Fred Uhlman *Spanish War* from Uhlman's *Captivity*
1946. Though some village priests supported the
Republic, the Spanish Church was generally identified
with Franco.

Nazi expulsion of Jews, depriving the nation
of much profitable stock: economics and
morality sacrificed to dogma.

Kemal died in office, not only from public
labours but from incessant gambling and
drinking. He had permitted an abortive
Opposition, 1930, but religious rebellions
did not tempt him to retain it. 'Let the
people leave politics alone for the present.
Let them interest themselves in agriculture
and trade. For ten or fifteen years more I
must rule. After that, perhaps, I may be able

to let them speak openly.' This could have
been Napoleon III but the Ghazi conceded
liberties only from a position of strength. He
seldom relaxed control of others or, on the
job, of his own harsh commonsense. There
may never be another Turkish Ghazi: this
is part of his achievement: that political
executions still periodically erupt, is another.
His career is disturbing, not ignoble.
Kemalism remains, an Atatürk Academy is
now to be established to study his teachings:
nationalistic, anti-communist, alternating
between repression and radical reform.

In anti-semitism, religion, capital punishment, free speech, sharp practice, humane
use of power, Left and Right too frequently
merge. Hitler, without complete farce,

claimed himself a socialist: Shaw, for whom intellectual activity was a passion vital as sex or art, came to admire Stalin and Mussolini, professional intellectual-haters.

Few have been more hated by 'the Left' than Franco, whose dictatorship, at least neither radical nor socialist, was anticipated by Primo de Rivera (1923–9) under the Monarchy.

The Spanish Republic of 1931 was concerned more with social rights and freedoms than with responsibilities and order, allowing debate, strikes, also destruction of churches, property, and other people. Violence is endemic to the nation rather than to particular parties. Long before even 1914 Barcelona was experiencing bombs, political and anarchist gangsterdom, gutted churches, assassinations. Party militia were organized: noisily on the Left, more secretly on the Right. Though granting religious and political tolerance, the Republic never wholeheartedly assaulted the privileges of Church, landowners, industrialists, and army. Like the Paris Commune, Mensheviks, Italian and French Left, it was disorganized by factions. Street fights, political murders, party vendettas evoked armed invasion by Franco as another 'Restorer of Order', excusably condemned by thousands of humble folk, less so by famous writers and savants busy praising Stalin.

Franco, a skilful, hard commander in Morocco, is still reviled for importing Moorish soldiers into Spain during three years of bloody civil war, though the Republic had already done so against rebels and strikers. Both sides used terror, though Franco continued executions long after victory, and kept the garotte, the traditional slow strangulation so unforgettable in Goya. Church and State repression have been strengthened: the régime shares with communists and Nazis the repression of national autonomists, educational dullness, strict political and industrial control, sometimes by military force which absorbs an abnormal percentage of national wealth. Old extremes of poverty and wealth remain.

Certainly, thirty unamiable years of Franco have shown a slow advance in agriculture, irrigation, reafforestation, industry, medicine: the growth of middle-class technology, affluence, capital assets reducing the notorious mass poverty. The Falangist bullies have been tamed, as Mao tamed the Red Guards. The early Falangist 'We are going to exalt national sentiment with insanity, with paroxysm, with whatever need be. Better a nation of imbeciles than insane internationalism', is no longer typical of Spanish thought.

Franco, though convinced of his own indispensability, is (1971) no 'Roman Emperor'. Not the Falange but the traditional monarchy is designated his successor. Stubborn, unimaginative, with streaks of viciousness, Franco is a solid realist. He broke his military oath to the Republic like a businessman cancelling an unsatisfactory contract. No expansionist delusions tempted him into further war. Once wanting to enlarge Spanish Africa, he has now almost abandoned it. After vainly pleading and threatening the Caudillo to enter the World War, as world conqueror, or victorious jackal, Hitler complained that he would rather lose all his teeth than renew such an ordeal, a deserved tribute to wily Franco, who had written, 'Historical Destiny has united you to myself and the Duce in a manner indissoluble.' He makes an occasional unlikely gesture:

> Although he accepted help from Hitler he gave refuge to thousands of Hitler's Jewish victims during the Second World War and revived citizen rights for the Sephardic Jewish community of Salonika, to save it from Nazi persecution.
>
> Brian Crozier, *Franco*

The régime is a prolonged, uninspired recovery from the million casualties of civil war, without the exuberance of Kemal, the

'Draner' (Jules Renard) *L'Homme à la Boule* 1870. Bismarck balances on the world; an authoritarian, but no dictator, Bismarck helped create conditions for a dictatorship which he did not foresee, and which would have appalled and disgusted him.

L'HOMME A LA BOULE PAR DRANER.

Tarteifle ! je ne gonprends pas ce que j'ébrouve ? Il me semble que je affre perdu l'éguilipre, et que mon pied il affre clissé sur la poule.

En vente chez STRAUSS. 7. rue du Croissant. & chez MADRE, 20, rue du Croissant.

943 — Paris. — Imprimerie VALLÉE, 16. rue du Croissant.

bray of Mussolini, though with the callousness of both. Dense with negations, it prefers 'Though Shalt Not . . .' to Nietzsche's 'Yea to Life'. In some areas, the State operates as an open protection racket. It thrives more on lack of coherent opposition than on stimulating policies. Benefits are grudging rewards for docility rather than acknowledgment of human rights. The Caudillo suppresses Catalans and Basques, as the Ghazi suppressed the Kurds and banished the Dervishes. Dangerous banked-down resentments at political and moral dogmatism, censorship, illegality of strikes make the future uncertain.

When Franco moves, one instinctively dodges. By suppressing the wider human energies such a government stores up malice, frustration, apathy, suggesting an unwholesome future. Literature is banished underground, or reduced to sententious platitudes, akin to Napoleon I's 'Courage is like Love: it feeds on Hope.' For most Spaniards, it could be much worse. No dream-pedlar, Franco, interested more in extending working hours than in envisaging the Great Holiday, does not in appearance or style remind them that it might be so much better. As in Maoist China, 'Help one another' also means 'Police Supervision'.

Napoleon III: a Classic Dictator

That he *is* a very extraordinary man with great qualities, there can be *no* doubt. I might almost say a mysterious man. He is evidently possessed of *indomitable courage, unflinching firmness of purpose, self-reliance, perseverance* and *great secrecy*; and to this should be added a great reliance on what he calls his *star*, and a belief in omens and incidents as connected with his future destiny which is almost romantic, and at the same time he is endowed with a wonderful *self-control*, great *calmness*, even *gentleness*, and with a *power* of *fascination*, the effect of which upon those who have become more intimately acquainted with him is most *sensibly* felt.

Queen Victoria

BADINGUET REVENANT DE LA GUERRE!!!

BADINGUET ALLANT A LA GUERRE!!!

What constitutes the statesman is a certain superior mediocrity.

Victor Hugo

The student of politics, Aristotle affirmed, must know somehow the facts of the soul. The Second French Empire almost glibly illustrates the diverse stimulants of dictatorship: the magical and spurious, musical and practical, racketeering and utopian. Born from dreams as by politics, dictators stand at the end of long troubling shadows.

Après le siege tenu dix-scpt ans,
Cinque changes ont en tel revolu terme:
Puis sera l'un esleu dc mesme temps,
Qui des Romains ne sera trop conforme.*

Nostradamus

The medievals never forgot Rome, France never forgot Napoleon's Empire whose cruelty and miseries time transformed to glamour, like a banker teaching money how to live. Dead hordes in Russia, youths hacking off thumbs to avoid conscription, Cossacks in Paris, became elegies, then anthems. People seem ever anxious to forgive enormities: history periodically reaches a lavish climax of misunderstanding rampant. By 1840, under colourless monarchies, the French imagination was becoming too solid. Bonapartism was the antidote. Napoleon, like Hitler, understood popular psychology, and knew that, if an army marches on its stomach, a people thrives on its memories, which can be manoeuvred, and even manufactured, by guileful generalship. His own

*The throne having been held seventeen years, five changes will happen in the same period. Then, at the same time, one will be elected whose policy will not conform too closely to that of the Romans.

Badinguet Allant à la Guerre 1870. Napoleon III as an ass.

mendacious memoirs made convincing propaganda. The Imperial glory revived in popular tunes. Balladry, almost as much as the Lie, is a Great Power, as in present-day Ireland. Napoleon I rated the *Marseillaise* worth an army corps. Dictatorship feeds on nostalgia. 'Memories are hunting-horns, whose sound dies along the wind.' (Apollinaire)

King Louis-Philippe (reigned 1830–48) tried to capitalize on this mood by bringing home to Paris the Emperor's body from St Helena (1840). At this posthumous Triumph, all flags, cannon, trophies, occurred an incident natural to incipient dictatorship. The white horse carrying the imperial saddle was, against all common-sense, yet, like a strip cartoon, half-believable, rumoured amongst the excited crowds to be Napoleon's original war-horse, Marengo. Under the same disturbing auspices, an astrologer, Madame Lenormand, foretold a Second Empire, a German invasion, Paris in flames (1841).

Revolution (1848) toppled Louis-Philippe, establishing a leftish republic bright with theories, sodden with inefficiency. Many hankered for a Second Empire as a second chance to identify with the most formidable name in French, in human, history. If only there were an available Napoleon.

Actually there was. Louis Napoleon (1808–73) was officially the Imperial nephew, though gossip, habitually unkind to women, questioned it. An elder brother, and Napoleon's own son, had senior claims but Louis was early convinced that he was chosen, had a star glittering for himself alone, essential ingredient for a world-ruler and which he accepted as a matter of course, without always knowing how best to use it. 'Who knows', the Emperor had said, 'that my family's future may not lie in this thoughtful child!'

Louis Napoleon was always thoughtful, the thought often opaque, streaming from conflicting sources. From Napoleon and Caesar, from his tutor Le Bas, son of a famous Jacobin martyr, follower of Robespierre, and from Saint-Simon, political

philosopher, later studied by Lenin, who envisaged the industrialized State managed by scientific élites and technocrats, revolving harmoniously and productively within a planned European order.

He was dangerously named, divided between 'Louis'—intellectual, 'sweetly obstinate', his mother said, lacking positive self-scrutiny but who could write that nothing founded on violence can endure— and the heroic, almost mythical, unscrupulous 'Napoleon'.

'Do you know, Fontanes, what amazes me most in the world? The inability of force to maintain anything at all. Only two powers exist in the world: Sword and Mind. Eventually Sword is always defeated by Mind.' Napoleon I's rather surprising words were more typical of Napoleon III. The nephew, as 'Napoleon', hankered, like the unmilitary Himmler, after authoritarian projects and warrior renown: he designed a howitzer and cannon, published an artillery manual, served as a gunnery officer in Switzerland, fought in an Italian nationalist revolt, began French involvement in Vietnam, commanded badly though successfully in one war, disastrously in another. As 'Louis' he enjoyed arts of peace, though not very wholeheartedly Art itself, failing to patronize Berlioz, allegedly slashing at a Courbet, permitting persecution of Flaubert. Like Prince Albert, who distrusted him, he devised Workers' Dwellings and Model Farms. He planned, from prison, a Latin American Canal and, from palace, assisted his wife's cousin, De Lesseps, in cutting the Suez Canal. He wrote copiously: on *Bonapartism*, reinforcing Napoleon I's 'Liberal socialism' with his own: on general politics, praising monocracy and social discipline: on economics, explaining how to abolish poverty: somewhat autobiographical history of Julius Caesar. No poet, he would have agreed with H. G. Wells: 'I write, like I walk, because I want to get somewhere.'

Alfred Lepetit *Le Porc des Tuileries* 1970. Napoleon III bids his star farewell.

LA CHARGE (Supplément nº 14)

Deuxième année. — En vente chez Madre, 20, rue du Croissant, et chez Duclaux, 21, place du Château-d'Eau

LE PORC DES TUILERIES, par ALFRED LEPETIT

(Dessin saisi sous l'Empire)

Adieu, mon étoile!

He has been despised as an adventurer: the adventurer is not despicable, society needs him as much as the conformist: though he implies amorality. Louis knew where he wanted to get. His star, after pale beginnings, waxed fierier. 'Napoleon II' died: the elder brother perished of fever in the Italian rising in which he himself was wounded. Through bribery he escaped from an Austrian prison. Later, like Hitler, he attempted a premature coup, actually two, the first ensuring deportation to America, the second, while securing him the publicity of a Paris show trial, ending in 'life-imprisonment' at a damp castle which permanently impaired his health. Here he fathered two children on a jailer's daughter, wrote his 'Mein Kampf', finally, after six years, like Mussolini but on his own volition, achieved a sensational escape disguised as a workman, Badinguet, a name with which his political enemies pitilessly mocked him throughout the Empire. Back in England, he knew Disraeli, who used him in one of his novels, cultivated rich women, enrolled as special constable during a Chartist scare, attended the Eglington Tournament, continued to train his Destiny until the great chance of 1848. 'A sad little man with a parrot profile and a gentle manner', he arrived in Paris with borrowed money and a Name. They were sufficient.

Like Hitler, he was a physical mediocrity: chain-smoker with short legs, stumpy flabby body, huge waxed moustaches on grey or yellowy face, heavy and impassive under shabby hair. 'The Emperor's head seems to have fallen on to his shoulders from a great height', the Goncourts noticed, Edmond considering that he resembled 'a circus artiste who has been fired for drunkenness'. For many he was always the dwarf who had filched the giant's clothes. None yet realized that he looked better on horse than on the floor. His low voice spoke several languages, each with the wrong accent. Again like Hitler, though more fruitfully, he was peculiarly attractive to women. 'There is something,' Victoria noticed, 'fascinating, melancholy and engaging which draws you

to him.' He remained the Silent, the Enigma, a mass of suggestions, or, as Bismarck said, a Sphinx without a secret. Napoleon I had dominated by force and gesticulation. Napoleon III impressed by dignity.

'In a novel the author gives some intelligence and a distinguished character to the principle personage. Fate takes less trouble: mediocrities play a part in great events simply because they happen to be there.' (Talleyrand) But in 1848, in the wake of three days of bloodshed and barricades, amid rampant oratory and measured insults, economic chaos and political hysteria, Louis Napoleon, however mediocre, deliberately planted himself there, acting with the restraint of finesse in a situation which was echoed in 1946 when De Gaulle declared that the case was hopeless, with the Left against the State and the Right against the Nation. He probably did not read Pindar, but would have agreed that 'the favourable moment is Sovereign of all'.

Once more like Hitler, and like another charmer, F. D. Roosevelt, Louis Napoleon was facile with vague though expansive promises to disparate interests. 'The name Napoleon is a complete programme in itself' was akin to Malraux's definition of Marxism as not a doctrine but a form of will-power. Elected to the National Assembly his speech was inaudible and his presence comical but the fiasco proved an asset. For the experts, he had collapsed beneath the weight of the Name. They thus permitted him to stand for the presidency against Lamartine (Laureate of the Girondins), and Cavaignac, successful, but only over the Paris streets. For those streets, and particularly for landlords, whatever else a Bonaparte represented, it was not anarchy or academicism. 'Poléon', 'Le Désiré', was elected overwhelmingly, for four years.

The French professionals of 1848 were no more alarmed than Krupps and Thyssen in Germany, 1933. Thiers spoke for them. 'Well, after all, four years will soon pass; my turn will come at the next election. Until then we will give the Prince plenty of women and lead him by the nose.' But Thiers had to wait until 1871, with 25,000 corpses lying in smouldering Paris. It was the mistake repeated, 1958, by politicians imagining that by recalling De Gaulle they could retain Algeria.

The Prince-President was either more or less than he seemed. His private beliefs would not have reassured either Thiers or the masses. 'The Nation is a slave who must be made to believe he is on the Throne.' His thoughts appeared to move slowly but they nevertheless moved. Throughout, he was both over-feared and over-ridiculed not for what he was but for what people thought he was. Mythology in action.

The Second Republic was a long skirmish between President and parliamentarians, the former looking past deputies to 'the People' of whom, as a tactical move, three millions were disenfranchized by the Right. Popular opinion seemed willing to prolong his term but the party leaders, aggrieved by the amateur's insouciant independence, were implacably opposed. When the Assembly rejected a presidential proposal he dissolved it.

No Bonaparte would meekly evaporate in 1851. He would exaggerate or invent terrorist conspiracies and constitutional intransigence. He would act, illegally, in the name of a Higher Law, defending property, majority rights, Motherland, order. On the night of 2 December, anniversary of Austerlitz, Louis Napoleon made his copybook *coup d'état*, almost a master-piece with its seizure of deputies and printing-presses, breaking of National Guards' drums, distribution of military largesse, mass proclamation of a *fait accompli* and guarantees against 'the Red Plot'. Later it was flawed by a panic massacre which the perpetrator was never allowed to forget; he would not have done so anyway, as 'Louis' agreeing with Nehru's words to Malraux: 'Even in politics an evil action has evil consequences. That, I believe, is a law of nature as precise as any law of physics or chemistry.' Occasionally Mussolini felt the same, fearing the dynamics of resentment.

Following 25,000 arrests, 10,000 deporta-

tions, a plebiscite granted the President power for ten years. Like Hitler, who also understood plebiscites, he swore an oath to the Republic he destroyed. This too was a risk.

But for a kingdom any oath may be broken:
I would break a thousand oaths to reign
one year.

Shakespeare, *Henry VI*, Part 3

On 2 December 1852, 'Le Désiré', backed by seven million plebiscitory votes, proclaimed himself Emperor Napoleon III, soon with a Snow-Queen Empress, an heir, 'the Child of Hope', a pageant-like court which Turgenev found 'ludicrous', but which many intellectuals mostly resented because they were seldom invited to it. He always remained the opportunist, the ringmaster concealing weakness with purposeful shows: flamboyant international conferences, exhibitions, buildings, parades, a constant flux of uniforms and horses. Like his latter-day successors he restored the Roman eagles. His pilgrimage with Victoria to the War God's tomb was magnificent professional theatre.

There I stood at the arm of Napoleon III, his nephew, before the coffin of England's bitterest foe; I, the grand-daughter of that king who hated him most, and who most vigorously opposed him, and this very nephew who bears his name, being my nearest and dearest ally! The organ of the church was playing 'God Save the Queen' at the time, and this solemn scene took place by torchlight, and during a thunderstorm.'

The thunderstorm itself seems part of the dictators' repertoire.

Unlike Stalin and Hitler, Napoleon III had no grudge against humanity. He wanted to improve its chances for pleasure. He had sense, sensitivity, kindliness, but his position as well as his personality held outstanding contradictions. Of his bizarre entourage he observed that only Persigny was a Bonapartist: that the Empress was a Legitimist, his half-brother Morny a Liberal, his cousin Prince Napoleon a Republican. 'I myself am

L'AIGLE DÉPLUMÉ!...

Alphonse Jacques Levy *L'Aigle Déplumé* 1870.
Napoleon III as the dethroned imperial eagle, wearing
a Prussian helmet.

Eduard Guillaumin *Polisson* 1870. Napoleon I
chastises his nephew for defeat at Sedan.

a Socialist.' Socialism, like Christianity, has various interpretations, notably by Napoleon III, Lenin, Stalin, Hitler, Tito, Castro, Mao. He exemplifies to the full the lineaments of the archetypal Dictator, for better or worse, the rise, achievements and fall, the fact and the legend, the awful, the tragic and the absurd.

Pacific, he was a Bonaparte: kindly, he was the Man of the December killings, as Mussolini was murderer of Matteotti. Liberal, but by origin and necessity an autocrat: irreligious, yet relying on Church support: rational, yet superstitious: nationalist, yet having to defend the Pope against his old advocates the Italian patriots: a supporter of foreign nationalism yet simultaneously also internationalist-minded, while ruling a people whose chauvinism turns deadly: progressive, wanting to conciliate the impoverished workers yet relying on the conservative peasants and middle classes. He encouraged Bismarck, who destroyed him. He is an object lesson in the dangers, indeed the fallacies, of personal power prolonged to excess.

Though at the supreme crisis, 1870, his moral courage failed, his normal stoic endurance was impressive. 'The risks of our profession', he remarked after Orsini's savage bomb-attack on himself and his wife, herself obsessed, aptly but unfortunately, with Marie Antoinette.

He too had grasping, untalented relations. 'You have nothing of the great Napoleon about you,' Prince Napoleon complained.

Honoré Daumier *L'Empire c'est la Paix* 1870.
Napoleon III had promised that 'The Empire means
Peace', yet indulged in expensive and finally
catastrophic wars.

'My dear fellow,' replied the Emperor with his subdued, rather endearing wit, 'you are mistaken. I have his family!'

His whole career, the books, relationships, reign, was 'almost but not quite', which is too often a requiem for a dictatorship. He helped free Italy but lost her gratitude for not doing more: to create independent Romania, who has forgotten him: strained to further friendship with Britain, who continued to mistrust him until his defeat made her vigorously affectionate. As 'Louis', sympathetic to trade-unions, as 'Napoleon' he dared not encourage them too far. He wanted a paternalist, stable, industrialized society of welfare, tourism, good times, that had also to find place for a Grand March.

The Second Empire had early successes. Industry was accelerated, trade expanded, money earned more interest, purchased more goods, in a prosperity perhaps unprecedented in France: notable railways, roads, canals were constructed; food and health standards improved: new towns were erected for workers and labourers: some rights to strike allowed: mutual-assistance societies encouraged: pensions and homes established for victims of industrial accidents. A Land Bank was established, often a gift of dictatorships. Paris was rebuilt, wide and opulent. The Emperor's cerebral fertility envisaged international disarmament, a permanent Peace Assembly, genial philistine happiness, Offenbach without the satire.

As debit, the violence, trumpets, propaganda postponed for a decade the obligation to think. National and local liberties were suspended. Like Mussolini, Napoleon reduced Parliament to a debating club, though not for always. Police spies in factories, *agents provocateurs*, censorship, intimidation of electors, Orsini's show trial to promote the Italian war, such was the other side of imperial amiability. More ominously, while thrilling fiscal and political schemes enriched the rich, real wages never increased quite fast enough to relieve the strains that so benefited the financiers, rentiers, middlemen.

Louis Napoleon had to escape the past, replace the name, which was mere magic and ultimately irrelevant, by energetic creativity, by the harnessing of modern currents of ideas, communications, commerce, science. More immediately he had to consolidate internal discipline, restore friendship with Britain yet eliminate the shame of 1815 when British, Prussians, Russians, occupied Paris. He had to abolish the Vienna Peace settlements as Hitler had to revoke Versailles. The deadweight of Austria and Russia must be shifted, so that romantic Poland, his ancestral Italy, and solid, industrious Prussia could breathe freely, even though not all of this might suit the true interests of France. Personally, he had to complete his uncle's career as Churchill had to complete his father's. And, like Churchill, who in Home Departments opposed armaments and in Service Departments demanded them, Napoleon was never bothered by consistency. He had always trusted to a mingling of fatalism and flair and, an incorrigible amateur, trusted too long. The Pretender was well served by the 'star': intelligent foresight and life-insurance would have better served the Emperor.

He did have a purpose, an Idea, for a new Europe, though confused by poor health, mental fluctuations, and the volatile mercurial French psychology. Like Hitler and Mussolini he lacked total mastery of whatever absorbed him. Always a little ahead of his time he desired intelligent cooperation between peoples liberated from reactionary foreigners preferably by his leadership and French resources. Nationalism was not the final end but a stage in individual fulfilment leading towards the peaceful unity of Europe, the World. The French themselves, particularly after the Mexican imbroglio, had reservations. Meanwhile, like Cobden, for whose statue in Camden Town, London, he helped pay, he believed in the civilizing virtues of free trade, signed a free trade treaty with Britain, 1860, despite unpopularity with French manufacturers. He was a distant prospector for the Common Market: had his Anglo-French schemes been more thoroughly followed up they would have secured him a base firmer than his last chimeras about Belgium, Luxembourg, Prussian alliance, Mexican Empire. 1860 also sent an Anglo-French expedition to Peking with barbarities that confirmed the Chinese hatred and contempt for the West.

The past's chief trap for a Bonaparte was necessarily military. 'Louis' had reassured Europe (1852), 'L'Empire, c'est la Paix', though 'Napoleon' fought wars in Russia, Italy, Algeria, Indo-China, Mexico, France itself. 'L'Empire, c'est l'Epée', the wits said. Mythology craved glory. 'Louis' could doubtless supply steady government—but so had Louis-Philippe. 'Napoleon' and large numbers of French demanded more. The Crimean War had to revenge 1812, reconcile Britain, gratify Christianity by succouring 'the Holy Places', flatter Paris by making her political Headquarters of Europe at the Peace Conference. Largely successful, he was to feel that at last he must intervene in Austrian Italy.

To the alarm of all but the Russians he had desired personal command in the Crimea. Against the Austrians (1859) his years of triumph allowed him his way and in a Franco-Italian campaign self-consciously Napoleonic but lacking a real Napoleon he did blunder into victory, then halted, too soon for the Italians but worried by European reactions and appalled at the Solferino carnage. 'I never knew it would be like this.' He had, nevertheless, freed much of North Italy, taking, for a tip, Savoy and Nice.

Still under his personal rule, the Empire, 1860, appeared solid enough, yet it never settled into being a matter of course, but remained only part of Napoleon's odyssey, or like a children's party in which everything must be manipulated by adults. Like many dictators he seemed more powerful than he really was. The nature of power itself is seldom obvious: *who*, or indeed *what* actually commands, decides, asserts, can be very questionable, and Napoleon III must privately have asked himself such questions. As the years crept over him with the malice of some ruined governess it became increasingly

UNIFORME CONTRE L'INCENDIE PROPOSÉ POUR LES CONSEILLERS MUNICIPAUX DEPUIS QU'ON BRULE LES HOTELS DE VILLE.

'Cham' *Uniforms Proposed To Be Worn Against The Paris Fire-raisers* 1871

a matter of debate, having, like many, perhaps most dictatorships, to be continually confirmed by official sensationalism. Napoleon had few talented colleagues: Morny, who might have kept the peace, Niel, who might have reformed the army, died too soon. Like his uncle, Napoleon had small faith in his own ministers, tending to act behind their backs with failing expertise. As his overworked body ran down, so did the Empire. France, though it had prospered greatly, was no longer disposed towards great gratitude. The urban masses saw no gain in unprofitable wars and rising taxes. The new Paris excited tourists more than it did the slum-dwellers of Faubourg Saint-Antoine.

The dictatorship was modified but concessions to parliament, press, unions, seemed extracted rather than freely given. Several prominent financial collapses at last indicated a dubious fiscal tone. Republicanism increased within the Assembly, led by Ollivier and Gambetta. Relaxed censorship meant the opposition not only of odium but of wit. France, jeered Rochefort, has 36 million subjects, not including the subjects for discontent. Anxious to move with the times, Napoleon appeared to be surrendering to them, his government a devious, complicated series of manoeuvres, though seldom altogether failing, his personal charm winning over Ollivier who, by 1870, was presiding over the last political experiment, a 'crowned democracy', the exhausted Emperor, not, perhaps, wholly unwillingly, entrusting many of his own powers to a cabinet responsible to Parliament. The heir was still a schoolboy, urban elections had shown frightening republican gains and riots in Paris. Workers and students scented blood. Putting a brave face on it the ageing conspirator staged a wily plebiscite which, despite emphatic rejection from the cities and sinister dissent from 50,000 soldiers, confirmed 'the Liberal Empire' by $5\frac{1}{2}$ millions that, in its last months, made opponents despair. The conjuror who had long seemed at a loss, after a row of failures too blatant to be disguised, had produced the rabbit from a hat indisputably his own.

The Empire ended as but one more of his 'marvellous adventures'. He had been seen entering Milan in a Triumph: seducing a countess planted on him by Cavour, tutoring the Child of Hope: as King of Algeria greeted by Arab chieftains charging almost to his feet: mechanically smoking at Tuileries balls, Italian battlefields: riding in procession between blue and silver Cent-Gardes or courageously driving out alone through seething, dangerous Paris, courteous, vulnerable, accepting with a half-joke Victor Hugo's gibe at 'Napoleon the Little', impassively listening for applause he was ceasing to hear, always solitary, deep in whatever was himself.

A political intelligence worthy of a states-man was hampered by the endemic suspicion of a conspirator by nature. Cautious and no lover of violence or bloodshed, he had also a fatalistic and passionate gambler's streak which led him twice unintending into war. The tragic irony is that, like Mercutio, he met disaster over a quarrel which was not essentially his own, which he tried to limit but could not in the end avoid.

Tom Littler (*Observer*, 11 June 1967) is describing Colonel Nasser yet the words drift back to the now dim New Caesar. Both were personally amiable, soft-voiced, sad-eyed, imaginative, restless, and having to balance personal inclination against the turbulent mob.

Very different from Hitler, Mussolini, Stalin, Mao, Franco, Napoleon III had known many countries and social classes yet his foreign policy derived from a curious, even culpable ignorance of foreign minds. Foreign policy is apt to ruin dictators, who cannot bend before a dark wind. While luxuriating in genial visions of their futures, he knew little of Mexico and Prussia. Likewise, Napoleon I dismissed the British as 'Lions led by donkeys', Hitler was misled about Britain by the vain and shallow Ribbentrop, Stalin was mistaken about Hitler and, perhaps, Mao. Though of finer texture than his uncle, Napoleon III had alarming, pre-Freudian simplicity, believing that votes were won in proportion to benefits conferred, that Bismarck's pleasant manners meant what they seemed, that foreigners

Eduard Renaux *Le Départ de la Commune* 1871. Disgusted by the pacific and moderate tendencies of the new Republic, 1870, the Paris town council, under a collection of socialists, idealists, anarchists and terrorists, declared Paris a 'Commune', independent of the Republic, the first of 40,000 similar French Communes. It lasted three months, under the eyes of besieging French republicans and German invaders. Their rule of terror included the murder of hostages, among them the Archbishop of Paris. In defeat they attempted to burn down Paris. The ensuing White Terror helped promote the myth of the 'Glorious Commune', adopted by Marxists, unfairly, as the Commune was more anarchist than communist.

would not resent or despise him for gestures on their behalf. He dangled between a multitude of half-selves within the War God's appalling shadow, his later policies touched by Hitler's self-description: 'I go the way Providence dictates with the assurance of a sleep-walker.' Attempting to liberalize the régime he nevertheless retained the odium of dictatorship while dispensing with its advantages.

The Mexican Scheme, 'the greatest inspiration of the reign' (Rouher), was designed to please not only Mexico but Britain and Austria, the Church, all French classes, and revive Napoleonic grandeur. Like many of Napoleon's ideas, it was logical, imaginative, if slightly freakish, but wholly dependent on two assumptions, both erroneous: that President Lincoln would lose his Civil War and that Mexico wanted a Bonaparte protégé, Archduke Maximilian, as Emperor. (Rumoured to be the son of Napoleon II, Maximilian was also rumoured to be the father of General Weygand.) Not for the last time financial and diplomatic experts failed their government. The execution of Maximilian, on orders of the Nationalist leader Benito Juarez, after whom Mussolini was named, announced at the Universal Exhibition (1867), the most ornate show even the Second Empire had presented, exposed Napoleon to hatred, ridicule, even dishonour and accusation of bad faith.

He fumbled as the pace quickened. Prussian victories over Denmark and Austria, though in accordance with Napoleonic nationalism, dramatically strengthened a traditional, not yet satiated French enemy neither liberal nor peaceful. Napoleon wavered between appeasement and resolution, open conferences and furtive proposals for further tips, 'territorial compensations', between good sense and the desperate. His mistakes and hesitations won no allies and alienated the neutrals; pretentious authority cannot survive on loss of nerve. Dreaming of the rights of other nations he seemed to the French to be forgetting his own. The energy spent on rebuilding Paris might have been better spent on frontier defences. For a Bonaparte he was strangely timid about urgent army reform.

War scares and violent threats from home and abroad may assist a régime, stimulate the economy, lull criticism, preserve national cohesion, but, as Hitler was to find, the enemy may eventually become not only real but overwhelming. As if a priest invents a god and, one noon, to his horror, the god speaks.

A Franco-Prussian political crisis in July 1870 over the Spanish succession, the first in which the Press had decisive voice, won a French diplomatic victory, yet insufficient for an inexperienced Foreign Minister and the inflammable Paris mob. Further guarantees were recklessly demanded from, of all people, Bismarck. Knowing the unpleasant secrets of his own army, secrets to the French more than the Prussians, the Emperor, now sometimes prostrate with illness, 'almost but not quite' withstood Cabinet indecision and street hysteria and kept the peace in his own backstairs—or shifty—way. 'When someone suggested the convening of an international conference to settle the matter the idea was enthusiastically taken up and greeted by the Emperor with floods of tears.' (Theo Aronson, *The Fall of the Third Napoleon*) But, like Mussolini, 1940, Napoleon eventually overruled his own commonsense. Bismarck's adroit version of new French demands made them appear insulting to King Wilhelm. In the subsequent uproar no Napoleon, however ill, could face accusations of cowardice. War was declared on Prussia with the usual frantic self-righteousness, appeals to God, denunciations of perfidiousness, patriotic howls in Paris and Berlin, less fervour in the provinces.

Bismarck completed French isolation by publishing Napoleon's earlier, foolishly autographed designs on Belgium and South Germany. The *Spectator* wrote, 'This war has no cause, no motive, no justification save the fear of Napoleon Bonaparte that without it his boy's succession would not be clear.' Deep down, 'Louis' must have known it was the end. At dinner on the last night of peace, despite guests, 'the food was eaten in silence, with no sound other than the clink of cutlery to break the unnerving stillness. Telegram after telegram arrived for the Emperor; each would be opened by an aide-de-camp and placed before him. Every so often the Emperor would look across the table to the Empress with a distressed look that tore at the heart-strings.' (Aronson)

Yet perhaps, as the last of 'Napoleon' trailed after his sickened star, perhaps he had a chance. A quick advance over the Rhine, victory to bring in Austria and Italy and abash the Left who preferred national defeat to a revived Empire; his body responding. *A Berlin* the mob roared.

> Partings are at all times painful, but it would be difficult to conceive any farewell more tinged with sadness than that of the Emperor and Empress on his departure from Paris. There are no two people in Europe who have played so prominent a part in history during the last twenty years as the royal couple whose fate hangs upon the result of the present war. When they meet again, if, indeed, they ever do meet, what an eventful story will have been told, and each line written in letters of blood! To France, though the issues are great, the war is but one chapter in her history; but to the Emperor and Empress it may be the last chapter in the record of their career. For him at least there is no future but in success; in drawing the sword he has thrown away the scabbard, he has burned his ships. That gay and glorious city which as with an enchanter's wand he has remodelled and rebuilt will either close her gates to the fugitive or welcome the return of a victorious leader. Bold as the Emperor may be to beard Bismarck in his power, it will require more boldness still to re-appear at home without his army.

> *Pall Mall Gazette*, 18 July 1870

Ambushed in the magic 'N', crippled by illness, Napoleon took personal command against the most successful professionals in Europe. Another fatalist, Tsar Nicholas II, was similarly to ensure disaster, 1916. There was added the ill-prepared and indifferently staffed army. De Gaulle was an exception to French disposition to rely more on élan than technology, Foch himself (1910) regarding aeroplanes as useful only for sport. Napoleon III in 1870 showed physical courage but neither skill nor élan: his officers were mostly paralysed by their superiors' incompetence which fearfully resembled betrayal. No dictator learns from history. Napoleon should have recalled more emphatically his generalship in Italy, where he destroyed all his own written orders, to save them from caustic historians. About to order retreat at Magenta he was informed that actually, he had won, without knowing it.

'Death is glorious, but surprise is profitable.' (Victor Hugo) French mobilization was a horrible muddle. 'The Army of the Rhine', equipped with maps of Germany, not always with much else, was swiftly losing battles in France, Prussian guns ahead, republican cat-calls behind. Zola has described it with irony and tragic awe: criminal disorganization, vital shortages, improvised irrelevant strategy, constant rain, bewildered infuriated troops obstructed by the wicked pomp of the Imperial carriages and yelling obscenities at 'Emperor Baggage' and his hapless son. Napoleon, surrendering command to Marshal MacMahon, forbidden by the Empress to return to restless Paris, trundled, unwanted and ignored, amongst demoralized soldiers who stared at him amazed, mutinous, or worse. The doomed march to Sedan seemed more for dynastic than military hopes.

Perhaps the Marshal was, after all, only a dutiful unenterprising soldier, excelling only in self-sacrifice. And the Emperor, no longer exercising command, was passively awaiting the fulfilment of destiny. They were being asked to surrender their lives and the lives of the army, and they *were* surrendering. This was the night of the great crime, the loathsome night when a nation was knowingly put to death; for from that time forward, the army was in desperate straits—a hundred thousand men were being sent to the slaughter.

Zola, *La Débacle*

Encircled at Sedan the French repeated superb, useless charges, not to win but to escape. Ex-dictator, without a policeman, ex-commander, without an army, Emperor without a capital, Bonaparte without eagle or star, he had within a few dreadful days become nothing. Painted, scarcely able to ride upright, Napoleon for hours vainly sought redeeming death until, Prussian guns pounding incessantly from surrounding heights, he asserted himself for the last time and ordered cease-fire. No white flag existed in a Bonaparte army, eventually a cloth was found. Bismarck demanded unconditional surrender. Zola depicts Napoleon's drive to exile through his savage troops, then the famished horses, maddened, demonic, thundering over agonized wounded and riven landscapes, and devouring each other: the epilogue muted but stark:

> All the train of the Imperial Household, the cumbersome, accursed baggage vans, had remained at Sedan, in distress behind the sub-prefect's lilac bushes. Those in charge were at a loss how to spirit them away, how to remove them safely from sight of the poor fellows dying of misery, so intolerable indeed became the aggressive indolence they had assumed, the frightful irony which defeat had given them. A very black night had to be awaited, and then the horses, the carriages, and the vans with their silver saucepans, spits, baskets of fine wines, went forth from Sedan with great mystery . . . journeying with muffled tread and rolling along the dark roads amid an uneasy shivering, such as attends a theft.

In Paris not a blow was struck for the Bonaparte Empire. Failed dictators, unlike kings, have no friends. There followed the Third Republic, Prussian siege, occupation of Paris, proclamation of the German Empire at, of all places, Versailles, Paris burning, like Berlin, 1945; Red Terror, White Terror. Deceived by too much gold braid the masses periodically yell for a sacrifice. The Paris authorities had to pay for 17,000 civilian dead, which helped poison politics for a century.

De Montherlant judges the French as the most inhuman in Europe, callous to the old, brutal to children, ungrateful to heroes, tyrannical at the least opportunity, compassionate only when people are looking. Napoleon III had never been quite a hero: though he believed that he would return and find a welcome amongst those whose hopes he had destroyed, he could not have expected forgiveness for Sedan, the loss of Alsace-Lorraine, the scandalous humiliation of Uhlans booming Schubert in the Champs Elysée.

He accepted catastrophe, not with indifference but with the stoicism of which Napoleon I was incapable. The dynasty was important, it was not all-important.

> No, I shall not defend myself . . . sometimes a disaster overcomes a nation of such a kind that it is justified in blaming it all, even unfairly, upon its ruler . . . A sovereign can utter no excuses, he can plead no extenuating circumstances. It is his highest prerogative to shoulder all the responsibilities incurred by those who have served him—or those who have betrayed him.

He had not finally been one of those whom Cicero described as possessed of inbred madness impelling them to feed on civil struggle and rebellion, or those others whose private affairs are tied together in such confusion that, rather than die alone, they prefer to pull down society in one general conflagration.

Napoleon III died, unrecalled, whispering, 'Tell me, we weren't cowards, were we, at Sedan?' Years later, his Empress allegedly read aloud, over the tomb of 'Le Désiré' and 'the Child of Hope' the terms of the Treaty of Versailles.

Sedan permanently extinguished the myth of 'N'—which survives only as decoration for London's Café Royal—though not the French need for saviours. De Gaulle, with his plebiscites and grandeur, recalls the

Corsican 'New Caesars'. In the Paris he rebuilt, Louis Napoleon has no statue, no street name, though an occasional bridge recalls a Crimean and Italian victory. His bones lie in England, without hope of Triumph and white horse. In Phnôm Penh, Cambodia, once part of the Second Empire's conquests, a statue remains: the head is now that of a local king, Norodom, but the body is that of Napoleon III. M. Sedantaire, the wits said.

Felix Régamey, *Entrée Solonelle de l'Empereur d'Allemagne à Paris* 1871. The Prussian king, Wilhelm I, as German Emperor, with Bismarck.

Part III The Attractions of Dictators

They ask so little. On one thing they are inflexible: that you hate all you love, and that you love all you hate.

Pasternak

Parnell came down the road, he said to a cheering man:
Ireland shall get her freedom and you still break stone.

W. B. Yeats

The hum of the printing presses turning forests into lies.

W. H. Auden

In its over-simplifications of man and society dictatorship cannot long appeal to reason.

From *Metropolis* 1927. The mob, in an industrialized century, craves goddesses and the spectacular.

It is poetry run to seed, part of what Dr Johnson called 'the hunger of the imagination that preys incessantly upon life.' Churchill recognized this when he queried the abolition of the German monarchy, 1918, as creating a dangerous emotional vacuum. Liberal democracy may do little to alleviate loneliness, hopelessness, death-fears swollen by royal and religious emasculation. Freedom can be unattractive to many raised in the safety of God, King, Father. Dictators in reply may harness the crowd's religious instincts, become totems, lifted from the earth and drawing all men after them. The Nuremburg Rallies were operas imposed upon Holy Communion.

For a child, 'no one's the same, especially me'. Too many adults, undermined by vague oppressions, feel they are insufficiently special. Vicarious or personal power can remedy failure. Himmler was failed chicken-farmer and teacher, Hitler failed artist, Kurt Franz, of Treblinka Camp, 'The Doll', failed boxer, failed musician, Goebbels failed writer, Goering a drug-addict. Seeking to blame others, they want to control others. Lack of talent gravitates towards harsh assertion and political noise. Rules, exams, hard work must be demolished, to let in a new Magician of Light.

Heroes, striding vast halls of sleep, reconcile opposites; a function of dream. Jesus proclaims death is life, Hamlet makes murder satisfying, Falstaff makes lies amusing, Don Quixote makes madness sanity in a confused world. Prince Mishkin's sickness becomes moral health.

As Hero, the Dictator enlivens static authority with fantasies awash with licence. He does not prate about balancing the Budget, he ignores the Budget, or steals from neighbours. Symbol of order he yet appeals to aggression and periodically indulges it. 'L'Empire, c'est la Paix', and Napoleon III redoubles his military costings. 'No more territorial claims in Europe', and Hitler conquers thirteen countries. By conscription and circuses he makes the common man part of the show, living in epic, though few epics end happily and no hero earns his living. Dictators win glamour by constantly burning their boats: it is prosaic to reflect that the boats are generally stolen property. As if in a sardonic display of wit they can combine Left and Right: Mosley regarded himself as Left. They sanctify the darker impulses: communists can wholeheartedly accept despotism on grounds that it will 'wither away'. Such theoreticians can see to the depth of sky or Marx but not to the ends of their noses. They can be simultaneously criminal and patriotic, national and socialist: anti-semitic, violent and intolerant, yet respectable. The Dictator assuages the fears of property-owners yet recklessly stimulates the reckless have-nots.

In social turmoil of defeat, ambush, hopelessness, poverty, anger, the Dictator is hero, tragic or omnipotent. 'Giving orders and obeying orders are identical.' (Sartre) A John of Leyden seems martyr for dynamic ambitions overwhelmed by the old gang, though he is secretly convinced that, deep in man, stronger even than glory, is a yearning to be stripped, scourged, mocked and crucified.

'It's blasphemy for you and yours to set a limit to human plans, because to do so is to set a limit to God. It is not the duty of a king to do good, not even to govern: but to Be, to live in himself all that his people are capable of imagining. To exist in God's room, to make God more visible. To be God. To endure and transmit all possible feelings. To hold out even to muddy serfs and oafish soldiers, to the beaten and cowed, the violent possibilities packed in their swinish natures and filthy hearts. The soul of Kings and the soul of their people are different and must be kept separate. Each sustains itself by contemplating the other. Sun and earth. I am the King and am worthy. All of you, despite your solemn words and hypocrisy, are feeding yourselves on your recognition that I am worthy and that you must do to me as you did to Jesus.'
Peter Vansittart, *The Friends of God*

The mind is swept by poets, but Goodness is

difficult to dramatize, Shakespeare's Macbeth enthralls more than the historical Macbeth.

Even in defeat, the loneliness of power makes tragic appeal. After Waterloo, Napoleon I sailed, a prisoner, into Plymouth, and was asked to show himself to the crowd. For twenty years he had been the arch-enemy, said by old ladies to eat babies. He had broken treaties, lied, slaughtered, wrecked a generation. Yet, when he appeared, short, stout, unemployed, every man removed his hat. A story that impressed Oswald Mosley. (*My Life*)

A Napoleon seems to refute the idea of man, like a bird or lemming, controlled by blind instinct and habit, or, like a clerk, dependent on remote, unreachable managements. Dictators promise to restore personality to a world of automatons: their careers add top-soil to imagination long nurtured on Oedipus, Odysseus, Theseus, Faust, Tamburlaine, Hamlet.

The malignant fascination of power was formerly blamed on repression, but the Permissive Society is not immune from hero-worship, intolerance, moral apartheid, self-importance, hysteria, authoritarianism and a frivolous conscience. Happy homes, exciting teachers, expensive universities do not automatically promote even common decency. If too much authority may assist delinquency, so may too little. Bertrand Russell found D. H. Lawrence, prophet of new loves and freedoms, 'a sensitive would-be despot who got angry with the world because it would not obey. When he realised that other people existed, he hated them.' Like Marx, Freud too came to insist on his own authority and dogma.

Neo-Freudians like Wilhelm Reich traced fascism and crime to sexual frustration; socialists blamed economic selfishness; Christians, sin. No single element seems decisive; no single class or generation culpable. It remains to be seen whether ancient cravings for power, domination, submission, will be transformed by the modifications of traditional family patterns, by communal living and women's equality—or strengthened by impervious world authority and corporations, without court of appeal.

Power plugs the generation gap. The Gestapo enrolled all classes and ages: old ladies and young girls sighed for Hitler, war veterans welcomed Mussolini, middle-aged academics safely dream of themselves as Red Guards. In a paternalist society the Dictator excites women: or, like the Syrian 'Assassin' (the Old Man of the Mountains) and Father Divine in their artificial heavens, hypnotize followers into obedience. Or he may be the Demon Lover, Dark Seducer, spiritual Dictator, appearing under any regime, at one extreme Gandhi, at the other Charles Manson in his harem-commune sustaining the weak, the stupid, the drugged, the atrocious. During his trial (1971) for several murders including the stabbing of a pregnant woman, he was described by a female accomplice as 'a god-man . . . he just seemed to generate this love. Some of the things he said seemed to be pure truth.'

Other convicted women quoted his song, 'There is no good, there is no bad, there is no crime, there is no sin,' a motto of the twelfth-century Assassins, 'Nothing is true. All is allowed.' Manson apparently taught that everyone is simultaneously God and Devil, that individual life is without value. 'If you killed a human being you were just part of yourself. So it was all right.' 'I felt he was the Messiah come again, he was the Second Coming of Christ.'

It might be interesting to test one's reaction to Orwell's review of *Mein Kampf* (1940):

Nearly all western thought since the last war, certainly all 'progressive' thought, has assumed tacitly that human beings desire nothing beyond ease, security and avoidance of pain. In such a view of life there is no room, for instance, for patriotism and the military virtues. The Socialist who finds his children playing with soldiers is usually upset; tin pacifists somehow won't do. Hitler, because in his own joyless mind he feels it with exceptional strength, knows that human beings don't only want comfort, safety, short working-hours, hygiene, birth-control, and, in general, common sense; they also, at least intermittently, want struggle and self-sacrifice, not to mention drums, flags, and loyalty-parades. However they may be as economic theories, Fascism and Nazism are psychologically far sounder than any hedonistic conception of life. The same is probably true of Stalin's militarised version of Socialism. All three of the great dictators have enhanced their power by imposing intolerable burdens on their peoples. Whereas Socialism, and even capitalism in a more grudging way, have said to people, 'I offer you a good time,' Hitler has said to them, 'I offer you struggle, danger and death,' and as a result a whole nation flings itself at his feet.

Wassily Kandinsky *Battle* 1910
© by ADAGP, Paris, 1972

The Twentieth Century

The reasonable man adapts himself to the world; the unreasonable man persists in trying to adapt the world to himself. Therefore all progress depends on the unreasonable man.

Bernard Shaw

It is a great mistake to abolish the death penalty. If I were dictator, I should order the old one to be hanged at once. I should have judges with sensitive, living hearts, not abstract intellects. And because the instinctive heart recognised a man as evil, I would have that man destroyed quickly. Because good warm life is now in danger.

D. H. Lawrence

I too believe that humanity will win in the end; I am only afraid that the world will be simultaneously transformed into one huge hospital where everyone is everyone else's human nurse.

Goethe

During the years of my youth nothing would damp my wild spirits so much as to think that I was born in an era when the world had plainly decided to erect no more temples of fame, save in honour of business men. The gale of historical achievement seemed to have died down for ever, so much so that the future seemed irrevocably delivered over to what was called peaceful international competition.

Adolf Hitler

Cherish all change, be fiercely devoted to fire.

Rilke

Though the twentieth century was unprecedented in the speed of discovery and revaluation, though Man leapt from the earth, he carried with him his ancient mind. Machinery and standardization actually reinforced his need for heroes, heavens and hells, golden apples, misty conquests, for gambles, celestial nonsense, and the extraordinary. One sees Hitler, brooding and wretched, submerged in huge, cosmopolitan indifferent Vienna, ignored, scorned: like a hidden fire smouldering beneath a vulnerable, richly decorated palace.

Colonial atrocities, the Paris Commune, the determinism of Schopenhauer, Marx, Freud, Spengler, shocked optimists for whom Man, experimental and free, had replaced the tyrant God. 'We no longer believe that reason controls life,' wrote Spengler, an influence on Hitler. 'We have realised that life controls reason. Life has no goal. Mankind has no goal. We witness the sublime aimlessness of a great performance. Ideas act irrationally, through the blood. Consciousness is a matter of indifference. Life is the Alpha and Omega, and life is devoid of all system, progress, reason. It exists simply for its own sake.' Man, after all, was no god but animal, played upon by instincts and passions that ridiculed his Napoleonic will.

Some panicked, followed Tolstoy and Gandhi seeking wisdom from illiterates, despising science, politics, machinery. 'Any reasoned intelligent battle against death— such as that waged by medicine—is unfortunate and evil in itself,' Tolstoy stated; and Masaryk was shocked by the condition of the Sage's peasants. Others withdrew into esoteric art, or would come to agree with E. M. Forster (1941) that humanity's best chance lay in apathy, uninventiveness, inertia. Forster is commended by C. B. Cox (*The Free Spirit*) for reminding us that life

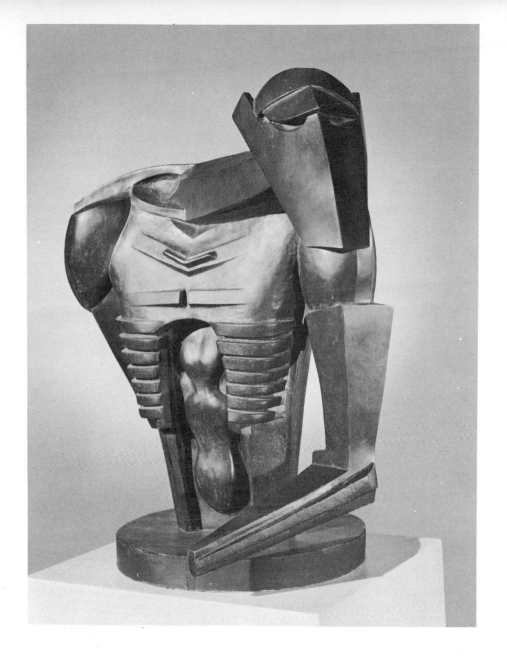

Jacob Epstein *The Rock Drill* 1913–14

is not composed from simple good and evil but from muddle.

Absolutes of Time, Space, Matter, Art, Cultures, Values, Morals were threatened by Einstein, Freud, Rutherford, Frazer, Bergson, Malinowski, Spengler, Picasso, Braque. Dream worlds were at one with day worlds. In new art and psychology the civilized was simultaneously savage, the primitive was exotic and sophisticated. The mind, like a collage from ancient Melanesia, or from Schwitters, incorporated novel and unexpected mementoes of pasts that were suddenly contemporary.

'Objection, evasion, joyous distrust and love of irony are signs of health. Everything absolute belongs to pathology.' Thus Nietzsche, whose works the Führer presented to the Duce: probably neither wholly understood them.

The mob had become citizens, but analysis

and education had not dissipated private disappointments and national grievances.

Not only children fear change. Atoms seemed replacing Providence but for many this was dispiriting; that they were not necessarily alternatives occurred to few. Novelty, or apparent novelty, alarmed, though much of it could have been found in Shakespeare.

Fernand Léger *Still Life* 1928
© by SPADEM, Paris, 1972

Freud discovered aggression even in jokes. In ferment of relativity, fragmentation, headlong experiment, older authorities in government, arts, morals, were clung to as totemic unities. Science, Modern Art were dehumanizing and complicated.

Scientific and economic determinism, however, after 1918, were to be mauled by forces more ominous than Tolstoy. Mussolini denounced 'the so-called scientific socialism of Marxism; the doctrine of historic materialism according to which the story of human civilization is only explicable by the conflict of interests between various social groups and with the change of the means and tools of production.'

Don't cant in defence of savages, Dr Johnson had urged, but the twentieth century, both stimulated and disillusioned by modernity, has sought Blake's intuition and wrath as much as reason and instruction. 'Intellectual activity has poisoned our people, the intellectual side of things disgusts me.' (Goebbels) For Himmler, 'Value will be placed on character rather than knowledge,' a view sometimes ascribed to British Public Schools. Cults of 'Blood' and anti-reason entangled such men of genius as D. H. Lawrence, outraged by complacent, polluting materialism and dried-up souls, and, of the Forsytes, writing that the more scholastically educated a man is generally, the more he is an emotional boor. For Bertrand Russell, spiritual descendant of Socrates and Voltaire, holding to reason, knowledge, clarity, precision, Lawrence was 'a suitable exponent of this cult of insanity'. His blood-knowing and sexual mysticism were 'frankly rubbish though I did not then know that it led straight to Auschwitz'.

In *Mein Kampf* the instigator of Auschwitz, attaching 'Blood' to Race rather than Life, ordained, 'No boy or girl shall be allowed to leave school until either has been initiated into the profoundest knowledge of the inner necessity and essence of blood purity.' What Hitler and a Nietzsche, Wagner, Lawrence had in common was not Race but belief in élites, passion, personality driven beyond limits. Lawrence wanted power over words, women, vision: Hitler, power over everything.

World Wars were in part the outcome of repellent cities. The physical dogmatism of conscription, suburbs, slum, assembly line, office routine, was as rigid as that of original sin and class war. Behind mean acres was somewhere green simple Nature, but Nature being violated by machines, trampled by listless hordes, smeared by uncontrolled Coketown. Human dignity, natural beauties, animals, were visibly debased for cash. Peruvians, Congolese, bludgeoned for rubber: blue and fin whales exterminated for oil and corsets: 15 million bison killed in twelve years. Himmler, shuddering at ill-treatment of trees, animals, soil, saw himself as restorer of rich, organic life, under the Swastika, archaic emblem of the purifying sun. That he could utter things apparently acceptable is a reminder that three men can say identical words, yet only one is speaking the truth. In 1912, the Russian poet, Blok, wrote, 'the sinking of the *Titanic* has made me indescribably happy: there is, after all, an ocean.' In *The Time Machine*, H. G. Wells, inspired prophet of technology, another Saint-Simonian, 'the Man who invented To-morrow', nevertheless presented a convincing nightmare of man perfecting his way of life and losing all reason for living.

An evil flower in the wasteland was perhaps better than no flower at all. A Kaiser praising 'the mailed fist', a Dictator trumpeting about Destiny, Blood, Soil, glowed with sublime simplicity. Democratic freedom repelled many long insured by God, King, Father; a sophisticate like Lytton Strachey could play with the proposition that civilization loves the truth, barbarism tells it. Authoritarian extremes of Right and Left profoundly mistrusted human nature: anarchists and pacifists perhaps trusted it too much.

W. B. Yeats was another prophet of instincts, interpreting history through mooncycles and reincarnations, passionate and impatient, with cavalier nostalgia for 'the old exalted life, the old splendour', which could perhaps be articulated politically. He could admire Mussolini and Franco who, like Hitler, were scarcely aristocratic but, the dirty work over, could presumably be replaced. Yeats spoke of the loss of delight in the whole man: blood, imagination, intellect running together. Hitler's 'the parliamentary decision by the majority sins against the aristocratic basis of Nature', would be acceptable to Yeats, Lawrence, Shaw, T. S. Eliot, whatever he might have proved to them in person. Mussolini despised human happiness as soft and stagnant, preferring 'a tragic and heroically agitated life'. As music it sounded well: translated into facts it destroyed life, including his own.

Genius felt itself suffocated by majorities: common man, ant-heap values tarnished the wayward vigours of life. Ruskin and Morris had vainly striven to make labour an art: Wagner and Carlyle raged against Man

stripped to an economic unit, and Wagner, who had known persecution and rejection, had hated, fought without scruple, won, was to fascinate Hitler.

Tribal instincts, individual excellence seemed endangered by international culture feeding on swollen cities. Eliot's eventual plea that 'to re-establish a vital connection between the individual and the race . . . the struggle, in a word, against liberalism,' parallels Hitler's, 'the highest aim of a folk-state is the preservation of those primitive racial elements which, radiating culture, promote the dignity of a loftier humanity.' Hitler conceived 'Nature struggling to bring forth an evolutionary higher stage of life,' a gloss on Nietzsche's 'Man is but a pretext for higher purposes, created to prepare for future Superman.' Shaw's disillusioned

From *Metropolis* 1927

Caesar reflects that, 'And so, to the end of history, murder shall breed murder, always in the name of right and honor and peace, until the gods are tired of blood and create a race that can understand.'

To such men, however different, growth of Europe's material assets assisted the growth of mediocrity. Prometheus, vital adventurous energy, was being frustrated by stagnation, rootless unpatriotic vulgarity, often, many intellectuals insisted, Jewish. Free Prometheus, and Life, Will, Genius would shake heaven and its static Zeus. Away with trashy lives, prudery, bureaucracy, conformist character-building, public conspiracies against the exceptional.

Down below, lack of recognition enflamed the neglected artist, intellectual sterilized by his own cleverness, desperate youth, criminal doctor, anaemic virgin, sun-seeking idealist, all wanting place, alchemical formula, godhead.

Mass-education can encourage but not invent talent. Indeed, by tantalizing with new and shining prospects and other worlds it may increase frustration, pernicious bewilderment, confusion of identity. An American student, July 1971, utters the old, ominous cry: 'Life is rapidly developing into a series of trivialities for me. It is a feeling as if I was in the rapids of a river and powerless to do anything except let it carry me wherever it will. There is a feeling of frustration at not doing anything of real significance or of value outside the narrow little slice of reality within which one moves.'

Such a mood may make it seem better to act, and act wrongly, than do nothing. Violence the precaution against too much equilibrium, or too much swamp. 1870–1914 could brood over aphorisms of professional non-combatants. 'Condemnation of War is absurd and immoral . . . ideas of peace can only assert themselves in times grown tired and soft.' (Treitschke) 'Condemnation of war is absurd and immoral.' (Hegel) 'To renounce war is to renounce life's grandeur.' (Nietzsche) 'Lasting peace, rather than war, tends to harden and bestialise people, generate cruelty and cowardice, fat egoism and,

above all, intellectual stagnation.' (Dostoievsky) 'War is the eternal form of higher existence.' Spengler, speaking for what some considered the higher nonsense. Sorel's appeal to violence excited Mussolini, became an intellectual cult. Shaw, genial, generous, wrote of the Boer War that he delighted in it more and more: 'It has washed the country out of its filthy wallowing in money; blood is a far superior bath.' Savants, musicians, explained war as an agent of Darwinian Natural Selection, though it selected those best fitted to survive. Idealists yearned to overthrow autocracy, imperialism, or recover provinces, at whatever cost.

In 1914, with troop-trains filling, ghastly fronts unrolling, overweight rulers blazing with unearned medals inspiring mass-ovations, Freud greeted the war with 'youthful enthusiasm', an opportunity for the libido. From the Left, Toller exclaimed, 'How glad I am that to-morrow I shall at last be playing my part, proving with my life what I think and feel.' Rilke, finest lyric poet in Germany, was momentarily back with Thor and Attila: 'Now it is you I will praise, Banner . . . you, now awake in battles, flaming with life like a bride.' And, 'Oh Mothers, the joy of giving! Give as though you were infinite! Give!' Rupert Brooke sang, 'Now God be thanked who has matched us with this hour.' H. G. Wells wrote crude war-propaganda. Thomas Mann, peer of Tolstoy, Proust, Faulkner, spoke of 'this great, fundamentally decent and in fact stirring people's war,' and again, 'It is not good when people no longer believe in war. Pretty soon they will no longer believe in many other things which they absolutely must believe in if they are to be decent men.' (Letters) The Socialist dramatist, Hauptmann, signed a manifesto justifying the invasion of Belgium. To Edward Thomas, future victim, W. H. Hudson confided, 'The blood that is being shed will purge us of many hateful qualities . . . of our caste feeling, of our detestable partisanship, of our gross selfishness and a hundred more. Let us thank the gods for a Wilhelm and a whole nation insane with a

C. R. W. Nevinson *Study for Returning to the Trenches*
1914–15

hatred of England to restore us to health.'

They forgot that civilization, like a rose, needs laborious care to nourish and preserve: it has artificial and precarious graftings, is fragile enough to be plucked, torn, thrown away, worn as a spoil, trampled. The inflated spirits evaporated on mounds of dead, maimed, ruined. Rich life becoming rich meat. For Ezra Pound:

There died a myriad,
And of the best, among them,
For an old bitch gone in the teeth,
For a botched civilization.

Winston Churchill reflected in *The World Crisis* (1925):

Torture and cannibalism were the only two expedients that the civilised Christian states had been able to deny themselves: and they were of doubtful utility.

They were to be tested further.

Millions died for a better world or survived into what was, for many, a worse. The fighting never wholly subsided. D'Annunzio, 1919, unofficially captured Fiume and was visited by an obscure admirer, Mussolini. Germany was black with private armies, the Freikorps—the future Nazi terrorist, Martin Bormann, was a member—wanting to retrieve frontiers or grab new ones, to retain loyalties, personality, action, in a dissolving world, to abolish defeat, avenge old wrongs, pretend that there was still an Emperor or that all were Emperors, above the Law. The novelist Ernst von Salomon, associate in Rathenau's murder (1922), describes 'their ruthless determination against armed or unarmed enemy masses, their limitless contempt for the so-called sanctity of life, and their disinclination to take prisoners under any circumstances.' (*Der Fragebogen*) Such spirit is not ironed out by sport, board-room, civilized discussion. Scarred by British war-losses, Oswald Mosley, war-veteran, international fencer, was to found British Fascism to, amongst other less wholesome motives, prevent a repetition. In 1970 the Japanese novelist Mishima, hungry for the beauty of the war-time suicide-pilots, killed himself after an abortive coup for traditional martial, anti-materialist purity and Emperor-worship. In *Confessions of a Mask* he had written, 'I began to love strength, the impression of overpowering blood, ignorance, rough gestures, ceaseless speech, and the savage melancholy inherent in flesh in no way tarnished with intellect.' To incorporate such force into civilization remains a task not always admitted and perhaps increasing.

While torture and atrocities screeched from Dublin to Vladivostok, there were also newer sounds, shapes, hopes, disappointments, in flux of idealism, brutality, morose jokes. Outraged by war horrors and profiteering, artists, intellectuals and publicity-hounds attempted to disown or disarm the guilty past, violate middle-class values—the moustache on the Mona Lisa, the perfect eye-ball severed—translate into myth and form thrilling vistas exposed by Freud, revolt, mechanics. Jazz, negroid dances, nudism, youth movements, open-air cults, tried to shatter the stuffiness of institutions, parents, clothes. Viler even than good taste was respectability. Bertrand Russell later remarked that no one can be respectable without being wicked. Marinetti (1876–1944) held a racing-car more beautiful than Greek sculpture: the socialist Richard Dehmel compared machine-guns to the music of the spheres. Kipling had belauded machines and technicians, found steam as soulful as sail. Apollinaire, futurist painter, master of Concrete Verse, had demanded (1913) 'originality, novelty, contempt for tradition', proclaiming sheer noise an art. Futurism was enthralled by speed, newness, flying: mindlessness, in crowds, or lonely above clouds, clamoured more than mind. Dada and Surrealism grimaced at conventions, even the greatest of all conventions, life itself. In Honegger's *Pacific 231* the machine turned

music. Le Corbusier planned houses as 'machines to live in' (1920). Cubism developed a sensuality of hard edges. In Léger's painting, man and machine fused in the harsh, pointed, tubular, gleaming. For Kandinsky, 'the impact of the acute angle of a triangle on a circle produces an effect no less powerful than the finger of God touching the finger of Adam in Michelangelo.' Another machine-addict, Wyndham Lewis, founder of Vorticism, wrote a book praising Hitler.

The Dictator too was a machine, lorry in a narrow way crashing through bicycles. Thoroughly dishonest lover, he stalked within metal imageries—Iron Guards, Steel Helmets, heading procession of tanks, shining belts and guns, glinting praetorian boots, the blare, tramp, relentless energy monopolizing the resonance of the universe, proclaiming the future yet also re-sowing the past, grinding down fears stirred up by startling or tormenting architecture, definitions of mind, painting. He was a direct stab into boundless intuitions. 'A violently active, dominating, intrepid brutal youth—that is what I am after. Youth must be all these things. It must be indifferent to pain. There must be no tenderness in it. I want to see again in its eyes the gleam of pride and independence of the beast of prey.' (Hitler, 1923) If to some this was the language of a frustrated spinster, to others it was from Alexander reborn.

Mussolini, Futurist devoid of art, after the Italian bombing of Barcelona, 1938, could at last rejoice that his people 'were horrifying the World by their aggressiveness instead of charming it by their skill on the guitar'.

The discontented, feverish, dulled, impoverished hailed the Dictator as priest in their midst, as Dionysus pouring sap and fire into life gone mouldy. Techniques of cinema, modernist painting and literature, industrial design . . . cutting, abbreviating, streamlining, montage, affected politics. Dictatorship was the short cut, 'to leap over centuries of slavery and backwardness and to by-pass reality itself.' (Djilas) Marching on Rome, slicing the Gordian Knot,

Giacomo Balla *Abstract Speed—Wake of a Speeding Car* 1913

liberating, from Mexico (1910) to Italy (1922), authoritarian revolutions erupted, breathless games without rules, with the democratic promise of a betting-slip, a Homeric nostalgia. Heroes were more important than whatever they represented: Pilsudski hurling back the Bolsheviks, Budenny leading Red Cavalry, a T. E. Lawrence, Richthofen, Goering, Guynemer, alike seemed knightly valour aglow in murky, fusty twilight, refurbishing individualism in a world standardized and meaningless, the world of such films as *Metropolis* and Chaplin's *Modern Times*. Fantasy and masculinity outbid the hangovers of the war: unemployment, Depression, topheavy millionaires, supine officialdom, national resentments. 'We should not bring about the Revolution to give power to a class but to give Life a chance.' (D. H. Lawrence)

International competitive sport and the cinema were manufacturing vicarious movement and freedom through heroes, paragons, lovers, Trojans, moon-goddesses, cut to fashion as cinema heroes. Napoleon I, Joan of Arc, Frederick the Great were further invested with the superhuman and supernatural, as Wagner's operas had invested Siegfried, and Meyerbeer, John of Leyden. The Dictator was another dream-image, prince and monster in one, goal-scorer, goal-keeper, more durable than actor or sportsman, more immediate than God. Capital letters, the Good, the Beautiful, the True were being analysed, then removed. The Dictator was one effort to replace them. Once more the Napoleonic promise that common men could soar, again the tumultuous love between centre and periphery, the escape from documents. 'I shall not rest until every German realises that it is a disgrace to be a lawyer.' (Hitler)

Mussolini gave an answer to Jung's *Modern Man in Search of a Soul*.

Fascism is Mussolini-ism. Let us not delude ourselves; as a doctrine Fascism

From *Napoleon* 1925

From *Modern Times* 1936. The workers bewildered and overwhelmed by a mechanical world, increasingly bloodless and meaningless.

contains nothing new, it is the product of the modern crisis of Man who can no longer remain within the normal bounds of life with its conventionalism, within the bounds of existing human laws. I would call it irrationalism. There is such a thing as morality but we are tired of it; I would go further and say it leaves us cold. That can be changed by swimming against the tide. We are a tormented people; each of us would like to be the sun, the pole of life for himself and for others. There you have the evil at the heart of modern man: call it irrationalism, Bolshevism, Fascism . . . Fascism, this storm of whirling souls.

Vigorous personality, the tug of life, was not monopolized by Dictators. Jaurès, Karl Kraus, Smuts, Churchill, Einstein, Roosevelt, Schweitzer, Gandhi also rejected mediocrity from a more generous excellence. Activists have always remained to whom, like Dickens, individual change of heart offers more substantial promise than a change of regime. They suspect those who demand power too strenuously, they consider that vileness remains vile even if it builds a dam or raises the school-leaving age: they dislike humbug. Chekhov rejected Tolstoyan archaism, the old man preaching sainthood and simplicity while remaining

From *Napoleon* 1925

From *Olympic Games* 1938. The Games were used
by the Nazis as political propaganda, but could be
seen by many, Nazis included, as an exercise in grace,
physical and spiritual movement. However, the
Führer's rudeness and ill temper at the success of
the US's negro runner Jesse Owens soured any
pretence of international goodwill.

133

Achilles Slaying the Queen of the Amazons 540–30 BC

famine, with Philip Noel-Baker rehabilitated a million and a half Greeks fleeing from Kemal. Such men were professionals, preferring hard work to slogans. They were not those of whom D. H. Lawrence wrote:

> People always make war when they say they love peace
> The loud love of peace makes one quiver more than any battle-cry

Nansen himself maintained:

> The politicians represented that barren self-sufficiency with its absence of any wish to understand other points of view, which is Europe's greatest danger. They called us fanatics, soft-heads, sentimental idealists, because it may be that we have a grain of faith that there is some good even in our enemies . . . I do not think we are really very dangerous. But those who are ossifying behind their political platforms and who hold aloof from suffering humanity, from starving and dying millions, it is they who are helping devastate Europe.
>
> Nobel Peace Prize speech, 1923

Nansen was proof that agnosticism can be as powerful as Faith, patriotism consistent with internationalism, that a puritan need not be bigoted or violent. He was continually driven by anger and pity to clear up the mess that others had made. When told a job was impossible he went out and did it. 'The difficult is what takes a little while; the impossible takes a little more.' As vehemently as D. H. Lawrence he rejected crowds as moral arbiters. 'The first great thing is to find yourself, and for that you need solitude and contemplation . . . Deliverance will not come from the rushing, noisy centres of civilization. It will come from the lonely places.'

Antoine de Saint-Exupéry, novelist-aviator, was no less heroic or passionate than Goering and Himmler, more aristocratic than Hitler, but less fastidious in his prejudices.

I think I could hit it off with these fellows [the Moors], without getting myself

despotic and complex. 'I myself have peasant blood,' Chekhov said, 'and no one can impress me with peasant virtues. I have believed in Progress since my childhood. Sober reflection and a sense of justice tell me that there is more love for humanity in electricity and steam than in chastity and fasts.' As much as a Lenin, Trotsky, Mussolini, the Norwegian explorer, statesman, humanitarian, scientist, sportsman, Nansen, 'the Conscience of Europe' Maxim Gorky called him, recognized the wastage of Europe and its efforts at Versailles to restore a dead era. He helped rally the League of Nations to eject Mussolini from Corfu, championed Armenian and Esquimaux minorities, organized wholesale relief during the 1921 Russian plugged. It's a risk worth taking. Not for the gratitude it might bring me—I couldn't care less—but for myself. Because I can't imagine some understanding not arising from a human contact, and because this is the only thing that has passionately interested me all my life . . . I feel there's a certain way of placing oneself on the same plane as others. And that if one doesn't understand other races, it's because one brings one's own vocabulary and categories of sentiment. Rather than a humble attention.

The Dictators demanded personal valour without often displaying it themselves. They are shamed by the Russian Elizabeth Pilenko who, after years of work for victims of Tsarist and Bolshevik cruelty, chose to take the place of a woman in the gas-queue at Ravensbrück: by the Polish Jew, Dr Korjack, voluntarily accompanying two hundred children to the gas, so that they should not die alone: by the Catholic, Max Kolbe, choosing to replace a condemned man at Auschwitz, then starved for a fortnight before being poisoned. George Orwell, fighting in Spain and coming upon a Franco soldier, momentarily becomes Dickens in action.

He was half-dressed and was holding up his trousers with both hands. I refrained from shooting him. I had come here to shoot Fascists, but a man who is holding up his trousers is not a Fascist but he is visibly a fellow human being similar to oneself.

Resistance is not inevitably violent. In 1940, in advice not unlike Bertrand Russell's, and which would scarcely have enraptured Winston Churchill, Mahatma Gandhi declared:

I do not want Britain to be defeated, nor do I want her to be victorious in a trial of brute strength, whether expressed through the muscle or the brain. I venture to present you with another and braver way, worthy of the bravest soldier. I want you to fight Nazism without arms. You will invite Herr Hitler and Signor Mussolini to take what they want of your beautiful island. If these gentlemen choose to occupy your homes you will vacate them. If they do not give you a free passage out, you will allow yourself, man, woman and child, to be slaughtered, but you will refuse to owe allegiance to them.

Jacob Epstein *Albert Einstein* 1933

Apotheosis of Unreason: the Nazis

Clutching a little case
He walks out briskly to infect a city
Whose terrible future may have just
    arrived.

> W. H. Auden

I will die leaping into my grave, laughing happily. To have had five million Jews on my conscience is an extraordinary satisfaction.

> Adolf Eichmann

They [the Germans] are always so badly deceived because they try to find a deceiver . . . Intoxication means more to them than nourishment . . . A popular leader must hold up to them the prospects of conquest and splendour, then he will be believed. They will always obey, and will do more than obey, provided they get intoxicated in the process.

> Nietzsche

It is a mistake to confuse strangeness with mystery.

> Sherlock Holmes

Intended as climax, Hitler has already become an epilogue. Abnormal, he was no mutation: he invented nothing: his New Order was Old Order at the wrong time, pushing out long-familiar prejudices with hysterical intensity and systematic ruthlessness. Similar forces were at work in Japan. National and racial chauvinism have been endemic to many countries since Biblical times or before. 'Let the Pope sell his rights to the French King . . .' Pierre Dubois wrote, 1300. '. . . it is the peculiar merit of the French to have a surer judgement than other nations, not to act without consideration, not to oppose right reason.' Robespierre

considered the French two thousand years ahead of all other races. 'It is tempting to consider them a species wholly unique.' Germans are not unique, though with an aptitude for difficulties; liable to extremes of self-pity, violence, musical thought disguised as political reasoning. 'The Germans,' Aldous Huxley considered, 'dive deeper and come up muddier than any other people.'

Cecil Rhodes—'Remember that you are an Englishman and therefore have won first prize in the lottery of life'—swindled and dispossessed the Matabele but stopped short of genocide, which General von Trotha used against the East African Hereros (1904–6). Herder, Schelling, Jahn, Hölderlin, Arndt, Wagner had philosophized about the Nordic folk-soul: developed with an air of science by Gobineau (France), Beveridge (America), and the Englishman, H. S. Chamberlain, who wrote to the Kaiser (1901) that 'God now builds on Germans alone.' Racial purity, *Limpia Sangre*, untainted by Jew or Moslem, had been insisted on by Spanish grandees for five centuries. Anti-semitism was a patriotic duty amongst ruling classes in Imperial Russia, Austria, Germany: Hasse, in *Greater Germany and Central Europe* (1895), advocated deportation of Jews and Slavs, annexation of the Baltic States, Poland, Ukraine, Ruthenia, Serbia, Romania. The nineteenth-century Austrian anti-semite, Georg von Schonerer propagated the Teutonic Racial Superiority that so affected Hitler and Himmler—as Kossuth had preached the Magyar Superman, Mazzini 'the Primacy of Italy', and Dostoievsky 'the Russian Mission'. It was a byproduct of Romanticism, making Wilhelm II's gentlemanly Chancellor, Prince von Bülow, write in his memoirs, 'Only horses and warriors guard

Josephine Crickmay *The Nazis Loved Nature* 1971

the steep height where the Princes stand. Not democrats, Jews, nor freebooters, for whoever puts his trust in them has built upon filth.' Of the Jews, the Kaiser wrote to Lord Grey (1907), 'There are far too many of them in my country. They want stamping out. If I did not restrain my people there would be a pogrom.' The Polish resistance, itself abominably treated by the Nazis, refused co-operation with Polish Jews (1939–45). Continuing Clausewitz's theories and anticipating *Mein Kampf*, General von Bernhardi (1849–1930) in *Germany and the Next War* condemned international arbitration, ridiculed treaties, demanded German domination. 'War, highest expression of culture, brings into play the loftiest activities of human nature. Individual crudities and frailties vanish before the idealism of the whole . . . Only when the possibility of war remains will national energies be preserved.' Hitler's Eastern policy repeated the ideas of Werner Daya, who (1918) imagined a conquered Siberia underpinning German agriculture.

The German Camps, reducing people to numbers, to clumps of hair, finally to nothing, were logical extensions of the poisoned, isolated bureaucratics of Dickens and Kafka, and even their enormities were not unprecedented. Twenty thousand Aztec victims were reputedly sacrificed at the dedication of a single temple at Tenochtitlan. The virtual extermination and emasculation of Red Indians and Australian natives were a disgusting precedent.

Of Hitler, Arland Usher has suggested that it was his sinister achievement 'that

Ashur-Bani-Pal, King of Assyria 668–*c*. 630 BC. The king fighting lions, both on horse and foot.

before him evil was always either half-hearted or shamefaced, hypocritical or stupid'.

Like Italy, Germany gained full unity only after 1870. Like Japan, it suffered the strains of rapid industrialization, and like Russia, wholesale military defeat (1918).

The Weimar Republic, between 1924 and 1929, made Germany a member of the League of Nations, produced useful housing, education, architecture, art, science, but failed to abolish political violence and tame the feudal Junkers, the industrialists, and officers' corps, or rehabilitate morale ravaged by the disappearance of the Empire and failure of World Revolution. Unimpressed by the League, many Germans saw their future threatened by inflation, unemploy-

ment, international distrust, street fighting, the Jews, urban sexual licence.

Weimar was insufficiently republican—only once, in the Right Wing Kapp episode (1920) was a general strike used—yet not monarchical. It connived at illegal flags and parades yet produced few of its own. Ultimately, the Papen-Hindenburg government prepared for dictatorship by Censorship, rule by Berlin decrees, without curing the malaise. Unemployment poisoned dreams. Bureaucracy was unshifted. Historians remembered the collapse of Rome: too many taxes, too few benefits. The situation was ominous for a people traditionally monarchical, paternalist, pedagogic, used to aggression and counter-aggression, swinging between boastfulness and inferiority. 1930, with over six million unemployed, brought a $6\frac{1}{2}$ million Nazi vote, though Hitler never achieved fifty per cent of the total franchise.

Dictatorship is loosely the culmination of

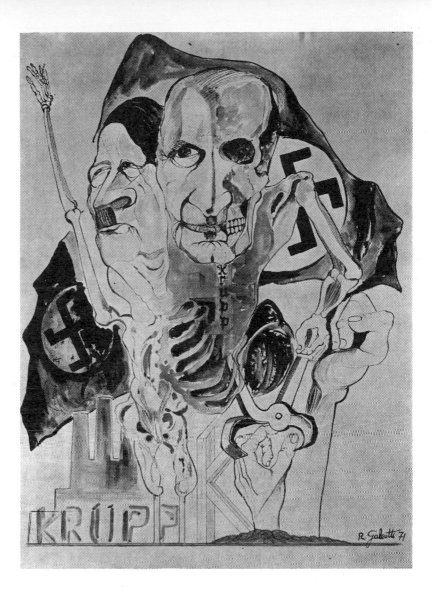

Renzo Galeotti *The Dwarf Giants* 1971. Hitler and
Krupp. The German armament firms, like others,
supported all governments save those who were
pacifist, and those were few.

wishful thinking, ignorance, error, plain
fraud. Nietzsche's Will to Power, lauded by
Führer and Duce, had implied self-mastery
for self-fulfilment, not brute conquest of
others, particularly by Germans. Hitler
bought support from financiers, Junkers,
arms cartels, Christians, atheists, war
veterans. The Catholic Centre Party, 1933,
voted with the Nazis to suspend the
constitution.

The German State had long connections
with industry. The Kaiser had been chief
shareholder in the nickel monopolists,
Frankfurt Metals, and had close relations
with Krupps, which itself owned important
Press interests. Hitler, as destroyer of old
classes, promised support for the small
trader against cartels and unearned incomes,
while accepting money from the steel,
banking, coal, chemical and arms bosses of
Rhine and Ruhr: Grauert and Krupps saved
him in a financial crisis, 1932. Krupps,
I. G. Farben, millionaires like Thyssen,
social figures like the ex-Crown Prince,
rallied to the Nazis. A stock Left diagnosis
(1939) was:

In Germany fascism came in February, 1933, as the immediate result of the temporary victory during the world depressions of 1932–3 of the depressed heavy industries of the Rhineland over the more progressive electrical and chemical and other similar industries, which in normal times did not wish to destroy the Trade Unions but to negotiate with them. This fact put at the disposal of the Nazi party large sums for working up the increasingly discontented and desperate masses, who were as hard hit as heavy industry by the crisis.

Patrick Gordon-Walker
An Outline of Man's History

Nazi 'socialism' promised to attack ground-rents and Jewry, promote workers'-control of industry, restore agriculture, resist over-urbanization, stamp out the Versailles Treaty, build half a million homes annually, cure unemployment. After electoral success, the Nazis' 'Enabling Bill' transferred Reichstag powers to Chancellor Hitler for four years. Through fear or actual arrest, all communists and some socialists were absent. Most socialists voted against, most Catholics voted with the Nazis. A massive plebiscitory majority confirmed the Dictatorship. Uniformed Nazis, smashing Jewish shops, were officially praised for 'doing the Lord's work'.

Economics do not control the unconscious. A programme of self-interest and scapegoat-hunting will not inevitably capture the total psyche. Contemporary British objections to the Common Market and loyalty to the Throne are as much emotional as reasoned. Diversity of human longings and culture, which the Nazis hated, was paradoxically their own saving grace. The better Nazis imagined a life both contemplative and active, fed but not corpulent, enriched but not wealthy. They believed, with Rilke, that Song is Existence. They revered the archetypal myths in Jung's Collective Unconscious, which momentarily deceived Jung into respecting them. Misguided anti-pollutionists, purgers of blood and soil, art and thought, they touched an ancient spiritual nerve of Goethian nature, uttered acceptable hopes, though with only part of their minds. Literal sun-emblems as well as swastikas adorned Nazi possessions.

Since 1870, as in Virgil's Italy, German farms had been deserted for cities, causing economic and emotional depression which particular Nazis sought to remedy. Deforestation and erosion were increasing. Cults of tree and soil were part of 'Germania'. The Forest, with its blacks and golds, sinister dusks and elvish light, is at the core of the German folk-tale. Hauerism, a twentieth-century German paganism devoted to Woden and natural fertility, interested Ludendorff, ex-war-lord, early Nazi supporter, increasingly mystical, like Himmler more pagan than atheist, both bemused by secret societies: Jesuits, Masons, 'Elders of Zion'. Here was a flashback both to heroic simplicity and to mystique: to heroes, golden suns, legendary mountains, blazing torches, eagled banners. The Nazi paper *Sigrune* attacked Jesus as 'a cowardly Jewish lout who . . . uprooted his disciples from blood and soil' and who finally 'insulted the majesty of death in an obscene manner'.

Hitler avidly accepted the ideas of Walter Darre, later his Minister of Agriculture, who desired a peasant revival to help restore racial and personal aristocracy as well as actual farming. Another disciple was Heinrich Himmler, dreaming of Nordic warrior-heroes, a German nobility forced by law to spend much of its time fostering its country-side. Puritan, practitioner of herbalist nature-cures, animal-lover, believing in sacredness of soil and hearth, hater of lawyers, with a collection of Jewish commissars' skulls as scientific evidence of a sub-humanity, Himmler was a devotee of Indian and Teutonic myth and, at the collapse, 1945, was clawing for enlightenment amongst Viking runes. The Waffen SS he saw as an Arthurian elite, moral, cultural, military, physical, racial. Seeing history in terms of heroes and devils, Himmler, confused by a muddle of selves, though behaving like a devil, was all too human. Richard Grunberger notes that Goethe's favourite oak-tree

Toddy Harman (aged 14) *Here Comes Mr A.* 1946. Painting done at Summerhill School, Suffolk, still managed by A. S. Neill, pioneer of 'progressive' concepts of education.

served as a pivot for Buchenwald concentration camp.

Hitler and Himmler were visionaries, conceiving a simple lost Nordic civilization of martial males and docile women, working and fighting under the broad leaf, corrupted and betrayed by dwarfish Hagen, by Mongols, Slavs, Jews. Himmler lamented 'the destructive Jewish spirit which caused European disunity'. He idealized his own role as destroyer. 'It is the curse of greatness that it must step over the dead to create new life. Yet new life we must create. We must cleanse the soil or it will never fructify. It will be a great burden for me to bear.' Of the mass-killings he added, 'All in all we can say that we have completed this painful task out of love for our own people. In our own selves, in our own souls, and in our character we have suffered no damage from this.' One hears again Robespierre, self-appointed Messiah, infallible, and recalls that the young Himmler, like the young Saint-Just, had helped the distressed; reading to the blind, fetching cakes for paupers, acting in a charity play for poor children. Such is the human fibre that at the trial of Ludwig Ramdöhr, hanged for murder and torture at Ravensbrück (1947), witnesses wrote of his delight in Nature. 'On country walks he would sometimes give small queer jumps to avoid crushing a snail or lizard.' Höss, Commandant of Auschwitz, hanged (1947) for mass-murder, a lover of literature, was 'friendly, courageous and unselfish', and would, as he put it, 'seek refuge from frightfulness and find peace among my beloved horses'.

Nazism was in part a reaction against science, the counter-attack of the magic, clairvoyant, supernatural still continuing in the revolt against technology, the computerizing of human relationships. Hitler declared that science had a shattering effect because it detracted from instinct. His impact jostled minds into an older time, bizarre, theatrical, but compelling. Superstition may obstruct economic and political movement while satisfying the emotional.

The Führer emerged not from Prussian militarism or aristocratic hauteur but from the despised and rejected: a demonic Messiah, god or nothing, with the language of Magic, which promises more than it performs. 'We must not ask if it is possible to attain this goal, but whether it is necessary. If it is impossible we must try it anyway and be destroyed. But if it is necessary and true, we must believe that it is possible just the same. And we need this faith. A thousand years look down on us, the future demands sacrifices of us.'

Famous Weimar films—*Cabinet of Dr Caligari*; *M*; *Faust*; *Dr Mabuse*; *The Hands of Orlac*; *The Blue Angel*; *Warning Shadows*; *Joyless Street*; *Waxworks*; *The Last Laugh*; *Secrets of a Soul*—may have helped prepare or reinforce an atmosphere of masochism,

imaginative inflation, defeatism, love of power: as if grisly wood-cuts and fairy-tales had come to life in a peculiar urban twilight of lurking murderers, uncanny fairgrounds, haunted people, charlatans, perverted school-teachers, astrologers. The Nazi leaders, in particular Himmler and Hess, were prone to astrology and mysticism. Richard Deacon (*A History of the British Secret Service*) suggests that Hess was lured to Britain by a fake horoscope planted on him by a British agent, emphasizing favourable prospects of a flight to Scotland 'in quest of peace', for

Paul Nash *Totes Meer (Dead Sea)* 1940–1. Smashed German planes after the Battle of Britain.

David Low *They Salute With Both Hands Now* 1934

David Low *In Future the Army will be Guided by My Intuitions* 1941

British pamphlet (1943) with spurious German imprint, containing fake Nostradamus prophecies. Cited in *Urania's Children* by Ellic Howe 1967.

10 May 1941. In Germany, the flight was officially blamed on astrologers. Goebbels used Nostradamus in his Psychological Warfare, the British countering with faked Nostradamus quatrains, commissioning the astrologer Louis de Wohl to post them with current German astrological developments, and assigning him to forge an issue of the German *Zenit*, an astrological journal. In 1945, Goebbels was imploring the Germans to trust the stars, which would save them.

The original Nostradamus had disconcerting ability to name, or near name, modern Dictators.

Of Spain:

De Castel Franco sortira l'assemble,
L'Ambassadeur non plaisant sera scisme;
Ceux de Ribiere seront en la meslée
Et au grand goulfre desnieront l'entrée.*

*Franco will expel the Parliament from Castile; this will displease the ambassador, who will break away. The supporters of Rivière will be in the struggle, and prevent entry into the great gulf.

Of Germany:

Bestes farouches de faim fleuves tranner;
Plus part du champ encoure Hister sera,
En cage de fer treisner
Quand rien enfant de Germain observera.†

'Hister' is mentioned thrice, once involved with 'a great one born in North Italy—to be ensnared by one clever at ambushing.'

Of the Duce:

Le Duc voudra les siens exterminer,
Envoyera les plus forts lieux estranges,
Par tyrannie Bize et Luce ruyner,
Puis les Barbares sans vin feront
vendanges.††

†Beasts, mad with hunger will make streams tremble; Hister will command ever-increasing lands; the great one will be dragged in an iron cage, when the child of Germany obeys no law, human or divine.

††The Duc will want to exterminate his own companions and will expel the strongest from the land, and by his tyranny will ruin it. Barbarians will then make vintage without wine.

I should like to put it on record that I have never been able to dislike Hitler . . . the fact is that there is something deeply appealing about him. One feels it again when one sees his photographs . . . It is a pathetic dog-like face, the face of a man suffering under intolerable wrongs. In a rather more manly way it reproduces the expression of innumerable pictures of Christ Crucified and there is little doubt that that is how Hitler sees himself. The initial personal cause of his grievance against the universe can only be guessed at; but at any rate the grievance is there. He is the Martyr, the Victim. One feels, as with Napoleon, that he *can't* win, and yet that he somehow deserves to. The attraction of such a pose is of course enormous; half the films one sees turn upon some such theme.

George Orwell, reviewing *Mein Kampf*

Toddy Harman *Solitary Confinement* 1946

Diffident and cunning, Hitler was a despot far different from Frederick the Great, Beethoven, Bismarck. He seemed emotionally stunted: lonely, prudish, friendless: a cripple yearning to lead the dance. His provincial childhood was divided between a harsh, embittered father, elderly, perhaps cruel, never very successful, himself illegitimate and lacking early love—and a mother much younger, mild and loving. The boy Adolf became inward, sly, determined to be not clerk but artist. Lop-sided child-parent relations are apt to excite fantasies of conspiracy, domination, fixation on leadership, evil minorities, Satanism. He was the epitome of countless lives frosted by ignorance and meanness, surrounded by wretched standards and ill-health: by dull air, small rooms, female sentimentality, cheap lodgings: by glum conformity, by remote, uniformed, unreachable 'They'. Sensations of inferiority and fear craved police, uniforms, guns.

Sexual deficiencies have been ascribed to Hitler and Robespierre, as to certain murderers, in some explanation of their lust to dominate. This may possibly underlie the noisy spiritual propaganda of Nietzsche, Carlyle, Lawrence. Kersten, Himmler's Swedish doctor, examined Hitler during World War II and found him syphilitic, suffering from progressive paralysis, with its by-products of delusions and screaming megalomania. He had already been treated, perhaps perfunctorily, for gas and blindness during World War I.

His pictures are dutiful copies. His writings and talk, issued with the devastation of complete sincerity, are a makeshift anthology of racial babble, popular superstition, pseudo-science, interesting speculation and half-history. He preferred newspapers to books, slogans to argument. The heat of his pronouncements recall a Caligula. 'If a people is to become free, it needs pride, and will-power, defiance, hate, hate, and, once again, hate.' (1923) The greater the lie, he wrote, the greater it will be believed, and he used it unsparingly in prodigious assault on international credulity. 'I shall give a propagandist reason for starting the war,' he told his generals (23 August 1939), 'never mind whether it's plausible or not. The victor will not be asked afterwards whether he told the truth. In starting and waging a war it is not Right that matters, but Victory.'

Odd Nansen *Death-gangs on their Way to Execution*
from Nansen's *Day after Day* (publ. 1949), drawings
done in Sachsenhausen and other concentration camps.

To A. J. P. Taylor, Hitler was 'a very
ordinary German', with a bleak vision of
'cities of concrete inhabited by hard Aryan
man and bound together by concrete roads'.
Home, slum, regiment deprived him of faith
in others: in generals, politicians, associates,
and, particularly the masses, whom he had
never known, in a Union, or in collective
civilian effort. He knew only the winter-
world of poverty, humiliation, despair. Three
years in a doss-house of informers, failures,
pimps, further years of rejection by arrogant
examiners, priests, officials, officers, meant
long horrors and sudden thrills, chiefly from
violent texts and Wagner's music. His father
had been a border-policeman, he himself,

briefly, an army spy (1919), neither job
generously motivated or likely to see humans
at their best. Begging for power, eloquence,
applause, triumph, he must have shared
Stalin's resentful mistrust of those who
already had them. There was nothing in him
of the large ideals and personal geniality that
could radiate from a Danton, Lenin, even,
at times, Mussolini. He was one of Auden's
'horrible nurses itching to boil their
children'.

Residue of an insecure, erratic, genetic
inheritance, dark winds roamed a mind that
could see itself as Hamlet without plot or
audience, victim of malign conspiracy from
those needing not saving but humbling. That
he was excellent at nothing suggested, but to
him alone, that he could be supreme in
everything. To master others was easier than
to master art, science, or make money, or
build human relationships. When he failed
an exam he came to feel that it was really the
examiners who had failed. Bound to thick
interior marsh his spirit would yet light the
sky.

Like a child, malevolent but wronged, he
had continually to make noises, interfere,
act, if only to destroy, reminding himself
and others that he alone really existed. He
was another who thought in 'music', though
with moments of insight that, dismissing
professional experience, at times seemed to
mantle him with the inspired and miraculous.
Probably never quite shedding that childhood self-mistrust, he made inordinate
claims on life that must often have left him
lonelier and more ominous, in both daydream
and nightmare, adder-country and flame.

A Hitler will interpret not only personal
failure but revolution, military defeat, world-
history, as the work of 'the system', or of
alien conspirators, to be resisted by enflaming
public opinion and arming the Chosen. The
would-be artist saw peoples as blank
canvases. With little understanding of individuals he had profound intuitions about
crowds, man at his lowest, pliable, hysterical,
ready to join a Gadarene rush towards
nothing.

Like Robespierre's, his effect on others was

elusive but startling. His radio voice hypnotized the Germans, his oratory made them gibber themselves into dementia. He was praised by the American air-hero, Lindbergh. Winston Churchill, scorner of Bolshevism and disorder, wrote (1936) 'If England found herself in the same situation as Germany, I would fall on my knees and ask God for a man like Hitler.' For Lord Rothermere (1934), 'The most notable figure in the world to-day is Adolf Hitler . . . one of a direct line of great leaders of humanity who seldom arise more than once in every two or three thousand years.' In 1939 he added that Hitler was 'a very great gentleman'. For Ezra Pound (1941) he 'taught the Germans manners'. Lloyd George was charmed by him. Lord Halifax found him

'very sincere, and Goering frankly attractive'.

Kersten asked Himmler if he would hang himself if Hitler ordered it. 'Himmler looked at me for a moment, shocked, then said, "Yes, certainly! At once! For if the Führer orders anything of this sort, he has his reasons. And it is not for me as an obedient soldier to question those reasons. I only recognise unconditional obedience." ' (*Memoirs*)

Here was the allure, diverse but spontaneous, not only of bare power, but of tinny music, a free drink, drifting perfume, handshake from a tall stranger, someone else's house in flames, a priest joking about hell, the stillness of a fortune-teller's waiting-room. Like a spin bowler, Hitler drew people forward, forced them back, left them

Odd Nansen *Waiting for the Cabbage Soup* from *Day after Day*

Odd Nansen *Neuengamme Camp* from *Day after Day*

Odd Nansen *Christmas Tree* from *Day after Day*

Odd Nansen *The Condemned Collected to be Shot*
from *Day after Day*

floundering, tempted them to fatal risks. Like a pop-star he transfixed the audience which, of its nature, responded to incantation not argument, 'happenings', not drama. But rhetoric has not yet built a home, achieved a masterpiece, surgical operation or scientific discovery. Nazism was a violent lack, a yell for everything and nothing.

Of the Nazi régime, Speer (1945) said it was 'only a soap-opera'. Gifted, fastidious, sensitive, Speer was one of those who, like a lazy or selfish lover, continually chose the easier course.

'Saving the State', Hitler broke it. The 'Thousand Year Reich' lasted twelve years. The 'Socialist' theme vanished. Science and education were debased: 'The Protocols of Zion' foisted on the schools and children encouraged to spy on their parents. Social services were manipulated for political means: national development sacrificed for Party and militarism: the cartels maintained and, though controlled by Four Year Plans, were strengthened by slave labour. I. G. Farben had criminal connections with Auschwitz: Krupps, by 1944, owned 138 slave camps and 100,000 slaves, paying the SS four marks for each Jew. Roads, re-armament, public works, enforced 'Winter Relief' cured unemployment in a policy that was to lose the lives of several millions of the employed and cause the partition of Germany for perhaps a century. Such feats no more justify dictatorship than Napoleon III deserves praise for fighting Solferino because it led to the founding of the Red Cross: or the Mongols admired because their invasions stimulated the spread of printing: or Philip the Fair's useful liquefaction of swollen Templar assets justified mass-killings of Templars.

The flight from the land was not arrested: human stud-farms produced no supermen. The war-effort was rotted by theory. Hitler could have used thousands of Russian deserters against Bolshevism but their 'racial inferiority' prevented it.

From the start, when heretics were thrust into Dachau, the regime was assiduous in the manufacture of pain. The SA Brownshirts,

the Nazi 'Left', were slaughtered wholesale, June 1934, by the SS, with the Führer, 'Supreme Judge of the German Nation', rival leaders, like the triumvirate in *Julius Caesar*, making their personal proscriptions.

The rest, 'the New Order', is an atrocious cliché: the gassings, hangings, shootings, torturings, castrations, starvings, over-workings. Bergen-Belsen has entered European demonology. Chronological time was ridiculed by the SS calculating how many Jews needed shooting to fill a crater of a bombed airport in Ukraine: by 33,771 Jews shot in thirty-six hours near Kiev. 20,000 could be gassed in a single day at Auschwitz. British troops entering Belsen, April 1945, found 13,000 unburied corpses, another 13,000 dying of typhus and starvation.

Above the gateway at Sachsenhausen was 'Work Makes Free'. Within was what Nansen's son, hostage for the Norwegian King, delineated (*Day after Day*, Odd Nansen). The yellow chimney of the crematorium vomiting stench; the gallows apparatus continually failing, the slumped victims having to have holes dug beneath them: gas-chambers and football matches: 'Honorary Teutons' queuing for Red Cross parcels while thousands of Ukrainians, Jews, gypsies starved in heaps or, at night, lay on corpses to keep dry; Christmas lamps illuminating the Tree behind the gibbet, loudspeakers blaring Strauss while naked, hairless bodies staggered through smoke pursued by whips and rubber truncheons.

At Gross-Rosen, the vegetables were fertilized by human ash: experts at Treblinka discovered that children burned better than men, less well than women. The garotte reappeared at Mauthausen, where victims were buried alive. Boy prostitutes at Auschwitz briefly served the Block Chiefs, then were killed, often with grotesque refinements. The Degussa Company melted down gold torn from teeth of the gassed. Thousands of clerks meticulously filed the deaths, providing mendacious causes. At Buchenwald, 3000 were infected with typhus, later kicked into excrement to drown. At Sachsenhausen men lifted the arms of the dead to receive extra bread, rootled and sucked in garbage, frantically ripped out the livers of dead gypsies. SS men hoofed the dying to see the reactions, played with strange favouritisms, surreptitiously commissioned children's toys from prisoners. The prisoners' orchestra at Treblinka played Offenbach. Dr Ekstein, at Auschwitz, a tragic wife-murderer, covered his wife's corpse lest she should catch chill.

After the Wannsee Conference, 1942, Adolf Eichmann, a relatively minor SS official, had been appointed to supervise 'The Final Solution'. Simon Wiesenthal, who, years later, tracked him down in Argentina, enabling his abduction to Israel, trial, in a glass cage, and hanging, wrote (*The Murderers Among Us*):

> I had been wrong to look for a motive in his earlier life. There was no motive, no hatred. He was just the perfect product of the system. When some of his underlings couldn't go on with the job of mass murder, Eichmann told them, 'You're betraying the Will of the Führer.' He would have done the same job if he'd been ordered to kill all men whose name began with P or B, or all who had red hair. The Führer was always right, and it was Eichmann's job to see that the Führer's orders were carried out.

The Waffen SS controlled twenty extermination and 165 labour camps. No party, class, religion or race can make capital out of the behaviour there. French doctors had denounced Jewish rivals to the Gestapo. Dr Korherr, 'one of the most hated SS leaders, was a devout Catholic' (Hohne). Mengele, mass-killer of 'inferior children' at Auschwitz, who, by injection and elimination attempted to breed a pure Aryanism, was Doctor of Medicine and Philosophy. Kuduk, of Auschwitz, who throttled the old by standing on a stick placed over their necks, joined the SS for 'the chess club, the comrades'. Communist prisoners volunteered to execute Social Democrats and Catholics: Jewish boards selected other Jews for slaughter: lawyers, artists, bank-managers, intellectuals, prim idealists, deranged thugs,

indifferent vagrants, manned the SS: Catholic feuded with Protestant. Nansen found Norwegians, enjoying special privileges as Aryans, adopting a Herrenfolk callousness. Prisoners could always be found to denounce, beat, hang, become camptrusties, extreme Left as eager as extreme Right. At Auschwitz and Buchenwald, the Hungarian Eugene Heimler (*Night of the Mist*) found the same. Hungarian prelates and bosses had preferred Hitler to their own socialists, Jews, gypsies: in the Camp, a Social Democrat refused to work with a Jew: while generously sharing his coffee with Heimler, a fellow-slave defended the extermination of Jewry.

Not all was predictable: there was individual courage, self-sacrifice, remorse. When a beating temporarily blinded Heimler, some prisoners stole his food, others fed him. People became scavengers, whores, saints, poets, or living zeroes. A peacetime pessimist, under Terror, turned radiant optimist: after liberation, some were merciless inquisitors. SS officers occasionally showed kindness.

The Camps pared the accomplishments of history. Established classes collapsed to whimpering hate, exhaustion, corruption: moral sense was extinguished in an underworld of scarcely conceivable time, present merging with past in unearthly hues, slaves regarding themselves as 'he' or 'it'. Silence, shadow, smell of the wind, were hideously distorted, magnified, embellished. Could one but survive, the tiny swelled to the enormous. The personality was a cell in which to dream of meals was substantial luxury, the sky's blue held infinite planes of richness, to pluck a leaf was extraordinary daring.

As a comment on the century, Sartre can write that the secret of a man is not his Oedipus Complex or his Inferiority Complex, 'it is the limit of his own freedom: his capacity for standing up to torture and death'.

Government, like teaching, is never an exact science, but a medley of art and intrigue, research and experiment, guile, insight and bluff, compassion and discipline, a balance between cliques and crowds. Dictators upset the balance, democracies tend to do nothing in particular, disdaining the emotions so crudely drummed upon by Duce, Führer, Lord Comrade.

Despite themselves, the Dictators suggest useful lessons: that personalities are dice, as liable to fly to horoscope as to computer: that democracy is not unworkable, but makes more exacting demands on the imagination: that eloquence is no substitute for wit: that standardization kills: that love-gone-wrong seeks redress in hate: that, in ever-growing populations, Liberty, as Clemenceau put it, is the right to discipline oneself in order not to be disciplined by others. And that, whether Left or Right, cringing is

inappropriate in human affairs.

Truth is secured by man: reputations are in the gift of Time, as wielders of power may be conditioned or transformed by Power itself. In September 1965, a BBC reporter asked a Kent schoolboy what he knew about World War II. 'My Dad's told me that Hitler was taking over a lot of countries, we went in and helped, but later he turned against us. So there was War.'

To be Lord of the Four Seas of China
A man must let men make verses,
He must let the people play comedies
And historians write down the facts.
He must let the poor speak evil of taxes.

Bibliography

I am not a specialist, and owe much to books and talks with my former teachers, J. Hampden Jackson, and J. M. Thompson, whose numerous works on the French Revolution should interest any reader who has reached this stage. In general, I have written from sources easily available to the ordinary reader.

Aronson, Theo *The Fall of the Third Napoleon* Cassell, London 1970
Auden, W. H. *Collected Shorter Poems* Faber and Faber, London 1950
Atkins, John *George Orwell* Calder and Boyars, London 1963
Camus, Albert *The Rebel* Hamish Hamilton, London 1951
Cate, Curtis *Antoine de Saint-Exupéry* Heinemann, London 1970
Cecil, Lord David *The Young Melbourne* Constable, London 1939
Churchill, Winston S. *The World Crisis* Butterworth, London 1925
The Gathering Storm Cassell, London 1948
The Grand Alliance Cassell, London 1950
Cohn, Norman *The Pursuit of the Millenium* Secker and Warburg, London 1957
Warrant for Genocide Eyre and Spottiswoode, London 1967
Cranston, Maurice (editor) *The New Left* The Bodley Head, London 1970
Crozier, Brian *Franco* Eyre and Spotiswoode, London 1967
Deakin, F. W. *The Brutal Friendship: Mussolini, Hitler and the Fall of Italian Fascism* Weidenfeld and Nicolson, London 1962
Deutscher, Isaac *Stalin* Oxford University Press, 2nd ed. 1967
Djilas, Milovan *Conversations with Stalin* Rupert Hart-Davis, London 1962
Field, Frank *The Last Days of Mankind: Karl Kraus and his Vienna Circle* Macmillan, London 1967
Fisher, H. A. L. *History of Europe* Edward Arnold, London 1936
Fromm, Erich *The Fear of Freedom* Routledge and Kegan Paul, London 1942

Grigson, Geoffrey *Notes from an Odd Country* Macmillan, London 1970

Grunberger, Richard *A Social History of the Third Reich* Weidenfeld and Nicolson, London 1971

Hare, Richard *Pioneers of Russian Social Thought* Oxford University Press 1951

Heiden, Konrad *Der Führer* Gollancz, London 1945

Heimler, Eugene *Night of the Mist* The Bodley Head, London 1959

Hill, Christopher *Lenin and the Russian Revolution* English Universities Press, London 1947

Höhne, Heinz *The Order of the Death's Head* Secker and Warburg, London 1969

Holroyd, Michael *Lytton Strachey* Heinemann, London 1967

Horstmann, Lalli *Too Deep for Tears* Constable, London 1951

Howe, Ellic *Urania's Children* William Kimber, London 1967

Jackson, J. Hampden *Europe Since the War* Gollancz, London 1959

Laver, James *Nostradamus* Penguin, London 1957

Malraux, André *Anti-Memoirs* Hamish Hamilton, London 1968

Manchester, William *The Arms of Krupp* Michael Joseph, London 1970

Mandelshtam, Nadezhda *Hope against* Collins, London 1967

Manvell, Roger and Heinrich Fraenkel *The German Cinema* J. M. Dent, London 1971

Minogue, K. R. *Nationalism* Batsford, London 1967

Moorehead, Alan *The Russian Revolution* Hamish Hamilton, London 1958

Namier, Lewis *Vanished Supremacies* Penguin, London 1963

Nansen, Odd *Day after Day* Putnam, London 1941

Nicolson, Harold *The Congress of Vienna* Constable, London 1940

Orwell, George *Collected Essays, Journalism and Letters* Secker and Warburg, London 1968

Pasternak, Boris *Doctor Zhivago* Collins-Harvill, London 1958

Payne, Robert *The Roman Triumph* Robert Hale, London 1962

Rees, David *The Age of Containment* Macmillan, London 1967

Runciman, Steven *A History of the Crusades* Cambridge University Press 1951–4

Russell, Bertrand *Portraits from Memory* Allen and Unwin, London 1967

Saunders, Edith *A Distant Summer* Sampson Low, London 1946

Schapiro, Leonard *The Communist Party of the Soviet Union* Eyre and Spottiswoode, London 1960

Shirer, William *The Rise and Fall of the Third Reich* Secker and Warburg, London 1960

Sieburg, Friedrich *Robespierre* Bles, London 1937

Solzhenitsyn, Alexander *The First Circle* Collins-Harvill, London 1968

Stalin, Svetlana (Alliluyeva) *Only One Year* Hutchinson, London 1969

Stendhal, H. B. *Rome, Naples and Florence* Calder and Boyars, London 1959

Talmon, J. L. *The Origins of Totalitarian Democracy* Secker and Warburg, London 1952

Thomas, Hugh *Cuba: the Pursuit of Freedom* Eyre and Spottiswoode, London 1971
The Spanish Civil War Eyre and Spottiswoode, London 1961

Thompson, J. M. *Louis Napoleon and the Second Empire* Blackwell, Oxford 1954

Toynbee, Arnold *Acquaintances* Oxford University Press 1969

Troyart, Henri *Tolstoy* Fayard, Paris 1965

Tuchman, Barbara *The Proud Tower* Hamish Hamilton, London 1966

Vansittart, Peter *The Friends of God* Macmillan, London 1963

Gordon Walker, Patrick *An Outline of Man's History* Plebs, London 1939

Wheeler-Bennet, John *George VI* Macmillan, London 1958

Wiesenthal, Simon *The Murderers Among Us* Heinemann, London 1967

Woolf, Leonard *Downhill all the Way* Hogarth Press, London 1967

Index